THE MONOLOGUE BOOK

Dialogues for One

Gary Wheeler

Copyright © 2013 by Gary Wheeler.

All rights reserved. No parts of this book may be reproduced, distributed or stored in any form whatsoever without prior written consent of the author.

FIRST EDITION

Actorsco
P.O. Box 98
Linthicum, MD 21090
gary@actorsco.com

Library of Congress Control Number 2013913544
ISBN-13: 978-0615846712
ISBN-10: 0615846718

Wheeler, Gary. *The Monologue Book: Dialogues for One.* Linthicum, MD: Actorsco, 2013. Print.

1. Acting 2. Drama 3. Performing Arts
   1. Title

Printed in the United States of America
by CreateSpace, an Amazon.com company

DEDICATION

All that I've learned about acting is from standing on the shoulders of three giants:

> Bill Blewett, my high school drama coach, who believed in a freshman.
>
> Wayne Shipley, my best man, who first taught me about film.
>
> John Strawbridge, my college film collaborator, who greatly contributed to my industry success on both sides of the camera.

A thousand thanks would never be enough reward for the view.

To Mark, Ruthann, Kacey, Jessica, Cori & Troy, for the words that matter most.

And especially to my wife Kathleen, who has allowed me enough air to soar and sufficient line as to not float away. Thank you always for your love and support and for not putting my bins outside.

ACKNOWLEDGMENTS

To the generous professionals who helped me flesh out a character and put food on the table:

Pat Moran, Dagmar Wittmer, Betsy Royall, Martha Royall, Scott Goodhue, Mike Lemon, Greer Lange, Donna Bellajack, Carlyn Davis, Craig Fincannon, Diane Heery, Kimberly Skyrme, Deb Docherty, Kathy Wickline, Jill Voran, Susan Allenbach and Brian Dragonuk.

And to all who have called "Action," including:

John Gray, Sydney Pollack, Ridley Scott and John Waters

v

CONTENTS

Forward	viii
Introduction	xviii
A Single Blueberry Pancake	2
A Simple Matter	6
Blah, Blah, Blah	12
Blue Alligators	16
Charity Begins at Home	19
I Probably Shouldn't Have Had That Coffee	25
Don't Say It	30
Don't Tell Me	34
Duty and Honor	39
Falling Soup	43
I'm Not Finished, I'm Just Stopping	49
It's Only a Drink	54
Jack's Adventure	58
Language Barrier	62
Roses for Rosemary	67
Single File	75
Sitting Down	81
Slating	87

Someday When You Dream About Me	93
The Confession	98
The Happy Little Girl	103
The Right Words	109
The Sense of it All	116
Thinking Ahead	123
Two Kinds of Men	129
When I Told Her	135
Would You Like to Dance	141
Afterward	145
About the Author	152

FORWARD

There's no such thing as a monologue!

Not the best way to promote a monologue book, but it's always important to define terms. If you're an actor, you're in the communication business. This book promotes effective communication. As such, the problem isn't with the material, but rather the approach that the term suggests. There, I've redeemed myself. It's not my problem, it's *yours*.

Now I will give you an out. You've been painted the wrong picture by other actors who've had the wrong picture painted for them. And since as a community we're very helpful, bad information travels as readily as the good. So let's toss out the painting and size a new canvas.

By stating there is no such thing as a monologue, I refer to the manner of performance. The monologue material exists and flourishes in dialogue. We just see and hear one side of the conversation and that conversation is not dependent upon a two-way verbal path. Even in the case of a soliloquy, the intrapersonal communication still reflects two sides-two minds if you will. As an audience, we need to see that dynamic created by the actor. In most cases, the audience should act as external observers and not participants (more on that later). Don't confuse a monologue with a speech.

Though certainly framed on communication, the lens of this book is not focused on speech communication. It is meant to instruct actors to develop and maintain a scene that will communicate something—most significantly that they can act. The audience will glean this information from an effective scene. This actually will demand more involvement on their part than if you simply handed it to them as part of a speech. And in most cases, the process will be much more enjoyable and memorable.

So by talking to the audience and thus opening the fourth wall, you may unwittingly find yourself looking through a wall that your audience has built to replace the one you've attempted to dismantle. Intrigue them and they will enter. Drag them in and they may run for the door.

What's the purpose of your monologue (not the scene)? Since you are required to have one prepared for an audition, the overall purpose is to demonstrate you. This allows us, on the casting side of the business, to make some determination about you. And even though much advice is given about selecting the "right" monologue, we could still do our job even if you picked the wrong one. Because it's not about the monologue, in this case, it's about you.

So what do we learn about you?

You establish a physical identity. We see what gender you are, how tall you are, your hair color (for those lucky enough to have some) apparent age (more important than actual age). Don't hide these things. Sometimes actors like to disappear in roles; however casting directors first need to know how you appear. Let them see *you*!

You establish a sound. What are the qualities of your voice? Do you have a viable dynamic range or is it a monotone delivery? Do you have adequate projection or are you difficult to hear?

You demonstrate movement. How do you walk? Do you glide, or float or strut or clomp? Aside from the affectations of the character, people have unique ways of moving. Start to watch people and you'll notice the subtle differences. You'll discover new nonverbal ways to communicate. Read those messages. Body language and movement speak loudly.

You hopefully demonstrate energy. We like to call it presence. We frequently can't define "it," but we know it when we see it. This connection we have with the talent doesn't have to be the result of a dramatic or overt expression or demonstration. In fact, the people who have "it," don't need to do anything to show it. I might add that if you are nervous at this point, that's a good thing. That's a sign of energy. We don't ride roller coasters because they calm us. If we didn't have a sense of anticipation, we wouldn't get on the ride. Enjoy that energy! Ask yourself for more. It will be your friend and aid your performance.

You will demonstrate your listening skills. That's right—your listening and reacting skills. The unseen character is involved in your dialogue. What are they saying? What are they doing? How are their reactions changing and or coloring your responses? You need to listen and help us "see and hear" that other person or persons.

Depending upon the monologue, the selection and variety of performance elements will change, but the necessity of their exhibition will not. You can still demonstrate these particulars regardless of the performance piece. And we can still recognize and categorize these attributes even if you did ten different "wrong" monologues. At least those of us who know what we're doing can do it. I say it that way because too many auditors are focused on the piece rather than the purpose.

Now is a good time to clear up another myth. Your character doesn't reveal itself alone. Your character is revealed through relationships and hence the dialogue. I'm always fascinated by people who insist that they aren't a particular way. Their sudden character flaw is attributable to a new experience or relationship, but they aren't really like that. The truth is that the flaw does reside in the character; it's just never been tested and thus previously revealed.

And now the final element: can you act? You knew we'd get there sooner or later. Why later? I've already seen a number of folks who can act. Maybe I have a hundred of your type. What I need is one little difference in the aforementioned that will make you more interesting and viable to the audience. Don't discount what you were born with or developed, as less important in the mix.

Let's talk about picking the "right" material. What will work for you? If you came out of a high school or college theatrical experience, you were probably afforded the opportunity to play many wonderful characters. I hope you enjoyed the experience. In the professional world, we now have actors who are age appropriate and type suitable to play those roles.

I know; you have range. In fact, it's your range that you want to reveal and extol. It's your range that will delight audiences everywhere, ultimately leading to that grand award. When you're an A-list actor, you can go for it, but even then I will ask you to look closely at performances. What you generally will see is not range but focused practiced nuances. I'm not knocking the performances; I'm only saying that once celebrity occurs, you will frequently observe the actor and no longer the character. As a director, I need you to do one thing—not many things. I have others who will do the other things I need. And when you win you're award (that's another book), you can say, "I told you so."

Common Mistakes

1. Attempted to demonstrate a quantity of acting rather than the quality.
2. Spoke to everyone in the audience (You are speaking to no one in particular and thus don't have a scene).
3. Spoke to one person in the audience (even if they liked it, that person is not your scene partner; he/she doesn't know how to react). Your scene is on stage.
4. Spoke over the heads of everyone in the audience

(Again, speaking to no one).
5. Too self-conscious.
6. The scene was too emotional.
7. They wrote their own material (see notes on that).
8. The character didn't go anywhere. No arc.
9. They worried about the time and rushed it (it's not a race).
10. They made the scene about the other character.

Make sure that you carefully attend to the notes for each monologue. Even if the monologue isn't to your liking or appropriate for your age, gender or type, the instruction is important to your mindset.

In some cases, I've asked questions that will offer clues to what I hope will be hidden treasure. In other instances, I've been more forward with my notes giving you specific insight into my thought process on the work. Don't simply prepare the monologue based on those notes. Consider them as you might a recipe, which is only one way to prepare a dish. You may find alterations that are more suitable to your liking and/or your dinner guests. You should still review these notes and deconstruct the thoughts. Whether I ask questions or give you specific direction, strive to develop the mindset that will help you with *any* monologue or scene.

What follows is a book of dialogues for one. If your dialogue partner is vivid, your scene will live. And always remember, the monologue audition is one of the few times that making a scene is a good thing.

Now go make a scene!

Gary

INTRODUCTION

Where do these monologues originate?

You would have to ask the more basic question; how do stories arise? The simply answer is that they are growing everywhere, waiting to be picked. Look and listen.

In several cases, I've included the origin within the notes but below you'll find other sources for my material.

Though I've suggested careful listening to be an important aspect for catching stories, even misheard accounts can provide viable inspiration.

"Charity Begins at Home" came from misunderstanding a story told by one of my students. When I asked her to repeat it, I understood what I originally heard was incorrect. But I found the mistake interesting, so I went with it and wrote that monologue.

Some of my monologues come from dreams. I have very vivid dreams and will use some of them for conscious exploration and though two of the monologues deal with dreams, neither one resulted from any nocturnal narrative.

I've written monologues from a passing comment, a song lyric, and a film or television plot. Sometimes a certain look will inspire a story. We all have stories and sometimes when they seem right out in front of me, I begin to write.

When I'm hired to write for an actor, I'll usually begin with an interview conversation. We'll chat and I'll observe. I'll watch demeanor, body language, gesticulation, wardrobe, hairstyle, facial structure and expression. I'm going to make a decision based on what I think is appropriate for your age and type rather than what you want to play. It will be more productive, though not always welcome. It's important for each actor to have a realistic sense of self. I may write about dreams, but as an instructor I'm interested in seeing you work. Know thyself! Once I was waiting in a cellular store and a customer entered. I immediately thought what a great face. He must kill people. I obviously didn't talk to this person (just in case), but if I were casting a project that needed an *obvious* killer, I'd cast this person. I'll worry about his acting later, if I even need to give him lines. That type of casting is called type over talent and it is very prevalent.

Of course, I've written about some of my own experiences, but don't believe everything you read. I do take license, add conflict and adjust the situation to hopefully create an effective story.

In recap, there's no single source or best option. Keep your eyes open and your ears attuned. And even if you don't see it or hear it correctly, somewhere in your path is a story.

Gary Wheeler

The Monologues

A Single Blueberry Pancake

No, No. I'll tell you exactly what I said. I said, "I want a single blueberry pancake." And she just looks at me, so I say, "I can order that, right?" Then she starts to write it down and says, "Honey, you can order whatever you want." So my buddy, Jeff and I are talking a few minutes and she comes back with our orders. And on my plate is a single pancake. But I don't see any blueberries, so I say something witty like, "Excuse me, but I don't see any blueberries." And she says, "Oh, it's in there." So I look at Jeff, who's looking at my pancake and he says, "Go fish." Naturally I ask her, "What's in there?" She says, "Your blueberry." I'm thinking out loud because this is kind of bizarre, "You only put *one* blueberry in there?" She says, "That's what you asked for." I tell her, "I asked for a single blueberry pancake." She's says, "That's right." I'm sure my pancake is getting cold, but I have to ask, "What's right?" And as though she got the question every day, she grins, "You got a single blueberry—pancake." I'm beginning to think am I on Bizarro World so with no attempt to hide my incredulity I ask, "You mean there's only one blueberry in there?!" Without any hint of disturbance she says, "That's what you asked for." I said, "I wanted a blueberry pancake. Just one pancake, but *many* blueberries." Pointing to my plate she qualifies, "Well that's a blueberry short stack." I ask, "How can it be a short stack when it's only one pancake?" She says, "You can't get any shorter than that...You want me to take it back?" Hoping to find my way back to Earth I say, "No, I feel compelled to look for my blueberry." So I kept it...And that's why it's on the coffee table. I figured it would be a great conversation piece, right? You have to go already?

Notes:

Let's begin this deconstruction by reviewing what we know. We know the other character has not been there long, at least in the opinion of the speaking character. "You have to go already?" Since the speaker refers to the pancake as a conversation piece, it is safe to assume we are in the speaker's home. Because the departure seems sudden and there's nothing scripted to indicate otherwise, it must result from either the manner of delivery or the idea of keeping a pancake to spark conversation. I will allow that a combination of both could certainly add to the reaction.

You must decide when this diner situation happened in relation to the newness of the relationship. On the surface, the relationship would seem to be new because the other character hasn't been there since the pancake came home nor has he/she previously heard the story.

Since he needs to identify Jeff, we can determine that the other character isn't Jeff. He also qualifies Jeff as his buddy, which could suggest at best, a minimal familiarity to the other character.

The success of this monologue turns on the last line. The story really isn't about the scene in the diner. For the actor's success, it's about the shift from relating the story to the honest disappointment by the other character's early departure. The story isn't meant to be a fabrication; it could easily be conveyed in a self-indulgent manner. If chosen, that would certainly provide greater contrast for the shift at the end. Given that decision, you also need to decide how the other character reacts to that manner of deliver, pancake shrine or both.

The audience will have a clearer understanding of the relationship at the end of the monologue. However when looking back, all the pieces must fit. The situation may have a twist, but the relationship must only have a reveal.

A Simple Matter

I'm sorry, but I can't be your friend anymore…Please, don't say anything, just let me do this…Part of me really doesn't want to do this, doesn't want to say it, but if I don't…I'm gonna friggin' explode…I know there's no way, no place, no time…that anything could possibly happen between us, but that doesn't change the way I feel…And I hate that. I hate that I've gotten to this point. I hate that I just can't be your friend. But I can't look at you anymore and pretend that when I walk out that door, I'm not gonna spend hours thinking about you. Friends just don't do that…I didn't ask for this to happen; I didn't plan for it to happen; I didn't hope for it to happen. It just did. And I can't explain it, except to look at you and say how could it not.…When I felt it start to happen, I even began to look for ways to stop it; to catch it before it got this far. I even made a list…Yeah, a list of everything that didn't make sense…that was pointless…even hopeless. And you know what the last thing on the list was? It doesn't matter. I actually wrote that on the bottom of the page—"it just doesn't matter"…The problem is *of course it matters*. That's the whole problem.

You…have begun…to matter…to me.

And I've lied to you. I've pretended that you didn't matter that much to me so that I could matter just a little to you.

I know by telling you this, I will have ended the thing I treasure most—the time I spend with you. But you're too important to me to keep pretending. And you're too important not to tell you what's crying inside of me…

…It's a simple matter of loving you. And I know that just can't be; it just can't be…

Notes:

Conflict drives story. Without conflict in some form, there's really no compelling engagement. Without conflict we simply have a time line of events. That may be important for some historical reference but it won't captivate an audience. Conflict may be bold and intrusive or light-hearted and modest. It is what drives us to distraction or gives us pause to think. Love may make the world go 'round, but conflict sets the pace.

The conflict in this story is obviously an internal one. The other character may be an unwitting accomplice or may be feeling the same way. The other character may have purposely driven you to this point or offer a way out. Regardless of the backstory you create, ultimately we'll see what you have let it become, so own it.

All we will see is the place where you've arrived. At

this point you are accepting the blame, if you will, for allowing yourself to get to this place. Perhaps there is some residual hope that despite your proclamation something may still be possible for the relationship. Perhaps you have accepted the thought that nothing will ever be the same and this relationship will now be lost to memory. Perhaps there will be some other turn of the screw. What we will see and know is the choice you made about this character in this moment. And what may be most telling is not in the monologue but how and where you look after finishing. That will tell us if there's hope or if all is lost.

Be careful about your emotional context. You will often get a more complex response from your audience by fighting the emotion rather than giving into it. We will enter the struggle with you. This is a particular problem for extracted monologues wherein the character exhibits a powerful emotional outburst. When an audience has taken the journey with you during a play or film, they can build to that place with you. The outburst is understood and accepted. However, if you were to walk onto a stage and then simply jump into an outburst, you have denied them the foundation of that structure. It's like an explosion going off. You got our attention but not our sympathy. Instead of invoking compassion, you invoke fear. The audience is trying to make sense of something and hasn't been allowed the opportunity to enter a suspension of disbelief mode. We simply don't believe it. You've probably seen these attempts. You may have heard these attempts from off stage. You typically have 90 seconds, so there is a competitive urge to show a quantity of acting in a very short period. Don't knock us over, take us with you.

It's important in all monologues to know where you were prior to beginning the piece. What was the initial condition or situation that led to the moment where the monologue begins?

One failure with a great many presentations is that

the scene begins right after the Big Bang. I'm sure it's not an intent, but unless the actor brings it from somewhere, unless the actor makes a choice, what results is "God made the heavens and the earth—action." With a play you know what's happened earlier. With an original monologue, you don't. You are given a snapshot and you must provide the answer to the question—what lead up to this scene? That is a challenge. That is work. Hopefully, that is exhilarating.

Blah, Blah, Blah

Blah, Blah, Blah. She used to say that all the time. Blah, Blah, Blah. It's not that I wasn't listening. I couldn't help but listen. All the time: Blah, blah, blah—*those exact words.* I guess maybe she thought it was funny. If she ever thought about it all…and I guess maybe I thought it was funny too—the first three hundred times. Of course everything is funny and cute when you're first starting out. Even blah, blah, blah. But sometime before Blah 4000, it started to get a little annoying. First thing in the morning—blah, blah, blah. Last thing at night—blah, blah, blah. I even started to dream about it. Not her—*it*! I'd be having this great dream about Heidi Klum and suddenly she'd say blah, blah, blah. It was just too much.

So you start to think, what's it gonna take to shut—her—up? And your mind starts playing all of these "what if" games. And the blah, blah, blahs almost becomes bearable, because you know that the end is near.

Fortunately, the jury understood. With time off for good behavior, I get out in three years…Peace and quiet. Do you know how precious that is? Do you know what that's worth? I'd tell you, but it just sounds like blah, blah, blah.

Notes:

What at first may seem somewhat innocent and typical, ultimately takes a much darker tone. I hope that will not be viewed as a typical male response. Throughout many classes, I've heard this delivered with a variety of pacing. The extremes tell a different story and both may work, but the voice I heard originally was the slow methodical expression of one of my students. It's akin to the vocalization that can't get out of its own way. As I have said, just because a writer hears it one way doesn't necessarily make that the preferred or best way. And despite your particular range, you will not likely find the opportunities in characterization as would a Johnny Depp. Yours will be a well-worn path, which is the more common mode of success. It may not be what you imagined starting out, but it can lead to little successes and theatrical longevity. With that said, your experiment with this piece will likely take you via your comfort zone. Stay true to that and the "twist" should work nicely.

Let me offer a word about the dark shift. Years ago, I watched Whoopi Goldberg performing one of her colorful characters. The piece was very entertaining and then suddenly the character offered perhaps too much information, which completely changed the tone of the piece. The character was still dead on, but suddenly the audience had to deal with a different tone. The pleasant laughter was swallowed by a sudden and uncomfortable quiet. It was a great performance with wonderful material. What would have been a simple pleasant memory about an enjoyable performance now had resonance that still rings with me today.

I am in no way comparing that wonderful writing with this piece except in the effect that such a shift can have. It's as if we are on an amusing path and suddenly the curtain is pulled back and we discover that we aren't where we thought we were. That's what you're working towards—pulling the curtain back and unsettling the audience.

Feel free to change the referenced female to anyone appropriate to your vision of the piece.

I've not heard this from the female perspective, but with some adjustments, I'm sure it could be highly effective. I hope that is writer's confidence rather than writer's conceit.

Blue Alligators

Okay, I can't get your panties out of my head, thank you very much. Now I know they'd probably be there anyway, but they'd be there on my terms and my time. If you're just going to bring them up whenever, then I'm not going to be able to defend myself—I'm going to have panties on the brain…okay, point taken. But you know, the more you try not to think about something, the more you think about it. And the more you think about it, *the more you think about it.*

Besides I do think about other things besides your panties…I do. Sometimes I think about blue alligators…I don't know, because they're not pink elephants. And that's a whole other story. Everyone knows you can't stop thinking about pink elephants. So—blue alligators…

Quite honestly, I'd rather be thinking about your panties…okay, maybe thinking isn't what I'd rather be doing...okay, blue alligators, blue alligators, blue alligators...don't interrupt me and don't say anything about your panties. Damn! Self-inflicted. Blue Alligators, blue alligators, blue alligators...

Okay, that's better. Now what were we talking about?
Blue ones?
Izod makes panties?
Blue Alligators—I'm so screwed.

Notes:

I think it's safer to dispense with the origination of this monologue. Your imagination will be much more entertaining than my explanation. At least that's my story and I'm sticking to it.

There are three conversational elements in this monologue. There is the dialogue he is having with the young woman. There is the dialogue he is having with himself as he attempts to right his thinking. And finally there is the unspoken dialogue she is having with him.

The fact that she is a young woman is likely the safest assumption that the audience will make. If you want to make her older, you will need to suggest that, however I think that's an unnecessarily challenging task. What is she saying? You'll need to answer those questions and hear the timing to allow for the correct pace.

Because the thoughts seem to be somewhat of a juggling exercise, the piece suggests a relatively quick pace. There is a struggle going on that the character wants to quickly bring under control. But alas, at least two balls seem to remain in the air. Don't you love analogies?

Have fun with the piece but don't get your Blue Alligators in a bunch.

Charity Begins at Home

Hello, I'm taking up a collection for the Benevolent Charitable Contributions of Mercy.

Not many people have. That's why we're coming door-to-door. We don't want to waste your hard-earned money on advertising. We'd rather put it right in the hands of the needy.

No—not the poor. We don't want to upset any government programs. No, it just seems fewer and fewer people are giving these days, so we're asking for contributions to foster and encourage charitable behavior. Could you spare a few dollars?

Well, the money goes to support our collection efforts. You know without us, people would probably stop giving all together. So we do this as our contribution to society. After all, charity generates a general feeling of well-being to those who freely give.

I know "charity begins at home," which is why we're stopping by your house today. And lucky for you—*you're home*. Now, if you're a little short of cash, not to worry. We'll be happy to accept a personal check or a major bank credit card.

Well you know sir, by the time that does freeze over, it'll be too late to give.

Now that won't be necessary because both of your neighbors have already called them.

Oh, is he sleeping? Because I didn't hear him bark when I rang the bell.

Please, let me save you the trouble. You can borrow my gun.

$50? That would be wonderful.

Thank you very much. Now don't you feel better?

Notes:

I have to confess that this monologue originated when I misheard a Working Actor student identify a charity whose name I thought was outrageous. I asked for the student to repeat the name and realized my mistake, but at that point, my mind was off to the races.

I've broken this monologue up because there's obviously an ongoing conversation with the unseen victim. The actor's task here is to allow the audience to discern the other dialogue through the responses of the actor. That means you'll need to allow enough time for the unheard response and non-verbal reaction on your part to keep the monologue from repeatedly slamming to a halt. Trust me; I've seen this performed haltingly on several occasions.

Despite the line breaks and the obvious nature of the responses, I never assume. This leads to my next admonition—read carefully.

On two occasions I've had actors arrive at the third to last line and say, "You can borrow my *gum*." Both times I let them finish and then retrieved their copies to check if I had misspelled the hand weapon I had intended. It was spelled correctly as "gun." My initial confusion was replaced with a new puzzlement, "What did you think the other person was saying or doing that would suggest offering them your gum?" One of the actors even pantomimed removing the gum from his mouth. So now I asked, "If you were giving them the gum in your mouth, why weren't you chewing it the entire time?" You have to know where you are going and where you've been. The mistake would have at least made some sense, if it were consistent throughout.

So what we have here is not a failure to communicate, it's a stickup. You have to decide why this person is going to all the trouble and time when all he/she has to do is show the gun and ask for the money. Now granted, $50 isn't a huge haul so why is such a small amount sufficient? Would the victimizer really accept a personal check or bank card? Is this really a perverted request for a legitimate charity? Are the police really coming? If so, then this person has ice water in his veins as he/she patiently proceeds with the patter. Is the character smooth or droll?

Now you may ask, "Will answering those questions really make a difference? Why can't I just say the lines? Won't people laugh anyway?" Yes; some people may laugh at the lines regardless of your choices. However there is a difference between appreciating lines and appreciating a performance and though I appreciate the former, your goal is to have the audience appreciate the latter. The audience will also probably recognize what is missing.

Allow me a physical analogy. Consider the CGI process known as performance capture. Plastic "jewels" are placed on the face to capture movement. Despite the number used, there are still subtle muscle movements not registered, which we see in the live human face. We aren't conscious of all of them unless they are missing. Someday we may be completely fooled, but let's not fool ourselves now. You need to do the work or we'll see what's missing.

You'll need to answer these questions and establish a workable tone for the piece. Above all, we need to hear both sides of the conversation in your delivery and response. Have I said that before?

I Probably Shouldn't Have Had That Coffee

I probably shouldn't have had that coffee. But I was really cold after drinking that Big Gulp. Of course now I can't stop talking, so I sure hope you feel like listening. I don't know what I'd do if you weren't here. I'd probably have to call somebody. QVC is always looking for callers. You know, people who have bought stuff and loved the products. I think right now I could even talk about that 100-piece set of fishing lures. Ever been fishing? Me neither. But what a great gift! I mean a hundred of anything for $29.95 has got to be a great bargain. You know what just occurred to me? I understand algorithms. Boy could I have used that in high school. I didn't understand much of anything back then. Do you think they try to teach you too much too soon? I mean maybe your brain isn't ready for high concepts until you're 25. Did I just say "high concepts?" I never knew there were different kinds of concepts before. This must be what infused knowledge is. There I go again. Are you getting all of this? Hey, maybe I'm picking up brainwaves. What are you thinking right now? No, really? It doesn't matter. It's probably just my brain expanding. Does my head look like it's bigger? That would be awful. Maybe I'm just accessing parts of my brain that have heretofore been untapped. Heretofore! Nobody says that. I must be a genius. What can I do with this newfound power? How can I help mankind? How can I relieve myself of this burden? How can I...find a restroom? I gotta pee.

Notes:

Routinely, I'll write monologues as one block of copy. I'll leave it up to the actors to place the breaks. I have a sense of where they should be, but as I've noted, I'm occasionally pleasantly surprised by a new interpretation. This however, is in essence, one stream of consciousness, which continually changes directions. There is the glue of self-amazement, but the wonder flashes quickly from concept to concept. Don't miss the clever placement of pauses. However even they must be driven by the caffeine intake.

I wrote this with a particular student in mind. She had a naturally fast pace in normal conversation, so I thought this would lend to that natural delivery. I gave her the monologue and it was the slowest she said anything the entire class. I've also had students attempt this at a faster pace without increasing their energy. That's just fast and flat. Some actors just don't have that gear. They think they're speeding along, but they're just cruising. Try as they might, they simply don't have a warp drive, which is not to say this has to be delivered quickly. It was my original intent and perhaps still the best, but I have seen an effective performance take it in the opposite direction and slow it down almost to an absurd rate.

Whatever your choice, commit entirely to that particular energy level and pacing. This is a "know thyself" decision.

Can you do it? Unfortunately acting is not like *The Little Engine That Could*. "I think I can, I think I can," won't get you over the mountain. You have to honestly *know* you can or select something else in your range.

When deconstructing this (or perhaps skipping that step), one mistake that novices make is to wait until the third sentence to establish the pace. In that sentence, you reveal that you can't stop talking. We need to understand that from the beginning. That should not be a surprise to us or to you.

Remember you will often find the keys to unlocking a monologue somewhere further into the piece. It is as though you need to read it backwards. For instance, the urge to pee does not magically occur at the end of the monologue. That should be indicated from the outset but probably not as an overt discomfort. When we look back, we should understand that you had to pee the entire time.

1. What is your relationship to the unseen character?
2. How are they reacting to your energy?
3. Where does this conversation occur? You make a reference to a restroom rather than a bathroom. You need to find one, which would indicate you aren't familiar with the location to know where one is.
4. Does the other character say anything? Just because something isn't scripted doesn't mean your interpretation shouldn't allow or include the unheard thought.

Don't Say It

Don't say it. I know what you're thinking. You think I'm cute. It's the naturally curly hair. Guys dig it and I spend hours trying to straighten it. You see, the thing is, I don't want to be cute. I want to be drop—dead—gorgeous. I want heads to spin like the lids on a jar of Vaseline Jelly. I want jaws to drop and not because my skirt's stuck in the back of my pantyhose. I'm tired of using that gimmick. I want guys to line up and not because drafts are 50 cents. Is that too much to ask? Seriously? Granted, it's not world peace, but I can wish for that once I'm drop—dead—gorgeous. And don't say it. I know what you're thinking. You're thinking "Honey, two more beers and you'll be Britney Spears." Well despite your newfound brew-inspired poetic forays, I am less than enraptured by your moronically self-acknowledged wit. The thing is, I don't want to be Britney Spears, I want to be me. I want to be appreciated for who I am. I want to be appreciated for my mind and every magnificent thought that proceeds from it. As long, of course, as I'm drop—dead—gorgeous. Now don't say it. I know what you're thinking. You're thinking you like a girl with spunk and personality. A girl who'll speak her own mind and not just every 28 days. You're thinking you like a girl with a little moxie. Just what the hell is moxie anyway? Well I've got that too, unless it's a skin disorder and that should go away in another week...So you like me. I can tell that about you, because you haven't gotten up and left like the other five guys who were sitting here. And you know something else? You don't say a whole lot. I like that in a guy—that and his...so tell me, what do you think? Am I cute? Don't say it. I know what you're thinking.

Notes:

I wrote this for a young actress on her way to the Big Apple.

Let's take stock of what we know?

1. She doesn't give anyone time to speak. That doesn't necessarily mean she's fast but she does maintain control and continues through what would ordinarily be the pauses in speech. I'm a big believer in the employment of pauses. Too many actors plow through material without placing any proper moments. Here, I'm suggesting you have to fill those moments with energy. You have to establish and maintain a continuum.
2. If she's already drop-dead gorgeous, there's a different issue that needs to be addressed.
3. She's scaring guys away. Why? Is it because she's not even cute? Does she talk too much? Does she talk too much about herself? What is the combination of elements and the degree of each that has this effect?
4. Is your character's hair supposed to be curly or straight? How would you play your hair's current condition against the answer to that question?
5. What type of character attracts guys by sticking her skirt in the back of her pantyhose?

6. She states that she wants to be "me." Given all of this information, who is she?
7. She begins and ends on the same line, but is she at the same place? Characters that don't go anywhere tend not to be too interesting. We like to see a journey; we like to see a change. Is there a change? If so, where does it happen? And how do you show it?

This actress was effective with this piece. One of the places in NY where she auditioned wanted to use it in their training sessions. That request would not have come back to me if she didn't do it well.

Don't Tell Me

Because we can't...we just can't. It has nothing to do with you. Well, it does, but it's not anything you did and there's nothing you can do about it so just go. Stop...Stop looking at me like that. See that's the problem. No...I don't want to talk about it. Because talking's only gonna make it worse. I know it's not fair; it's not and I hate it. Will you stop looking at me like that? Like that! You never used to look at me for more than a second. Now I can't look at you...Because you look at me like that! And we can't go on with one of us not looking at the other. It'll confuse the waiters. They'll think we're married. Not that that would ever happen because...we can't be friends anymore. Okay? Because sooner or later one of us is going to say it and then that's it. It's out. You can't take it back. You can't say you were just kidding. That would break one of our hearts. I can tell...Because you look at me differently now. Differently than how you used to look at me. I don't know when it happened. I just know it happened and that's why I can't look at you. I don't know what I'm trying to say. Except one of us is gonna say it if we don't stop seeing each other…I'm not mad; I just don't want one of us to say it. So please go. And don't turn around. And don't tell me you love me. Dammit! I asked you not to tell me that…You didn't?

Notes:

This is not love at first sight. This is a love that has been growing slowly and perhaps unevenly as one of the friends realizes that they are about to cross a line. My original design was that this was a female perspective, but it could easily be played by either gender or any sexual orientation.

Though the unseen character could be perceived as crossing the line, we discover that the speaking character is the one who has definitely gone further with the relationship.

Here are the questions you must resolve:

1. Is this a same sex or opposite sex relationship? There may be different constraints that apply. For instance in an opposite sex relationship, the question may arise regarding the viability of a male-female friendship? This question was broached in *When Harry Met Sally*. I use the scene in one of my film classes.
2. Are the characters single or are they involved in other relationships?
3. Why would changing the relationship be a bad thing?
4. Does the speaker really want the other person to go or does he/she want the other to admit an analogous set of feelings?

Regarding question #4, relationships are sometimes like gin (the card game not the drink). You throw a card down and see if your opponent picks it up or ignores it. You make what is essentially a vague comment without pointed meaning. How does the other person react? Does he/she respond in kind or ignore it? If there is a response, perhaps you next say something less vague. Does he/she respond, ignore it or shut it down? You play this game until you've established the relationship. Hopefully, it is the relationship that you want and that works.

Could the above dialogue be a card game? The relationship most assuredly will change. Perhaps the speaking character needs it to change one way or the other. Even though one result may be painful, it will be less painful then pretending that something doesn't exist.

The most important moment is of course the end. I don't say that routinely or as a matter of fact for all monologues. I will say in this case, it is the reveal. How will you say, "You didn't?" Are you surprised? Are you mad at yourself? Are you playing the moment like a card in gin? How will you look when it's out?

Will you look at the other person? Will you look down or up or away? Perhaps you'll use some combination of several beats I would be wary of the last choice as it may be confusing to the audience and read as trying too hard to communicate your intent. Keep it simple but know what choice you have made. That will tell us what your character believes and what they want. Therein lies your connection with the audience and their degree of engagement.

Duty and Honor

Don't call me that! You lost that right when you walked out. And don't tell me I'm an adult and should be able to deal with it. I shouldn't *have* to deal with it because *you* should be dealing with it. You know, you're the one that always talked about duty and honor. What was *that* about? Was that just for everyone else? Was that just part of our general orders? Because that's bullshit! You don't think this should affect us. But this isn't just about you. This is about all of us—who we are...or who I *thought* we were. You don't think this changes anything but an address—this changes *everything* and every one of us...Oh, don't even try. I don't want to hear any sorry explanations...So who is she? Men don't jump ship unless there's a port in view. You taught me that. So who is she? Obviously not someone who knew about duty and honor. And I guess she really loves you. She *understands* you. Maybe she's even better at taking orders. Is that it? Because what I do want to know is, what was all *this*? Was it just an act? Was a family a requirement for promotion? Was our whole perfect picket-fence-life a pretense to make admiral? Because if it was, well then, job well done, sir. But let me pin this on your chest. You know the greatest gift a father can give his children?—to love their mother. Next time you polish your brass Dad, remember the medal you're missing.

Notes:

This monologue resolved from conversation with a student and some subsequent assumptions I had based on that dialogue. In hindsight, I'd have to say those assumptions proved their share of insight.

The difficult task here, as is the case with any monologue in which the actor's character is upset with an unseen participant, is not to make the monologue about the other person. Again, the monologue must always promote your talents and abilities. The audience's relationship is with you and not with someone who isn't present. If we care more about them, you'll likely not be high on the list for a callback.

Questions you'll need to answer include those attempts by the Admiral to interject. What does he say? How does he react? You'll need to know that so you are in fact reacting to him (gender assumption though not a requirement) rather than just saying words. Your words really are secondary to how you feel. Has your character (not you) been practicing this scene or is this coming out as an eruption? Which process is more effective?

Another thing to be careful about is the emotion at the beginning of the piece. It's very easy to fall victim to the tirade. Though I've written it elsewhere, it's worth repeating; I've seen many monologue performances attempt to begin on an extremely emotional note. A problem for most audiences would be that abrupt emotional entry to the scene. We may feel uncomfortable, disbelieve it or even laugh because we don't know where it originates. In most cases, it fails. Be careful about thinking you're the exception; you can make it work because you are such a fine actor. There are differences among ability, confidence and self-deception. Reality shows make a fortune highlighting those with the latter conceit.

Be sure to weigh your options carefully and seek out critical guidance. Make some choices and ask if those choices have been achieved. You need to know if you're doing what you think you're doing. I've given direction to actors who believe they are making the changes, until they see the video. They assure me that they were feeling the change. Over the years, I've grown progressively disenchanted with what an actor feels; I'm more interested in what an actor communicates. Those things are not necessarily connected. Listen to interviews and judge for yourself.

Falling Soup

Errands. I love running errands. There's something so mundane about them. Don't you love that? There's no looking over your shoulder. Anyway, I was out running errands on (thinking pause) Tuesday. I had to drop the kids at school and then I went to the cleaners and the bank and finally the commissary. I'd gotten most of what I needed and headed to the soup aisle. The kids said they wanted soup. I'm not sure whose kids they are…It must be some commercial they've seen. So I'm standing there looking at all of the soup cans and I can't find anything. I mean, I see the cans but I can't see the words on the labels. Then out of the corner of my eye, I see him coming. He's pushing a cart…a wooden cart…he…looks very nervous; he keeps looking around but he's coming at me. He looks scared I think, but determined. I start to move back and reach for my weapon. I hit the shelves behind me. I hit them pretty hard. Things start falling but he's still coming. I can't find my weapon! I look back for a second at the soup and there's red everywhere and I hear someone yell. I...see red everywhere and I...I hear someone yell. I'm on the floor pushing hard against the shelves and I can't find my weapon. Where's my damn weapon?! Them I see them. There are people lying everywhere. I hear their voices; I hear a child crying. And then the man stops; I can vaguely see him and he's saying something to me. His mouth is moving and he's looking right at me and then I hear him say, "Are you all right?" (looking around) I start to look around and he says it again only this time it sounds anxious but more normal, "Are you all right, Miss?" I look down and I'm on the floor; soup cans are everywhere and boxes of cookies are lying on me. I look back up and people are all around looking down at me. There's a little girl sitting in a cart crying. Then someone in a white shirt and tie bends down next to me and asks if I'm okay...I said, "I need to get some soup for my kids." (uncomfortable pause) I think I need to go back, but I don't want to go back. I don't want to leave my kids again. I can't let that happen again. I can't see the soup falling with my kids there. I don't want to see those faces and all that red. I need to fix this. (fighting through her tears and shaking her head) I want to re-up.

Notes:

Post-Traumatic Stress Syndrome can manifest itself in seemingly mundane events through the process of transference. The original stimulus is replaced by another, resulting in a similar response.

I heard an Iraqi War Veteran comment about some confusion he experienced in a grocery store. He couldn't clarify his mind over a simple shopping task. With that story in mind, the above fictitious scenario explores what happens when a veteran no longer feels the safety of the commonplace.

For those who haven't experienced an extremely traumatic event, a day's ordinary events may seem exasperating. There are so many little tasks obliging us to time that we'd rather spend doing something else. For those asked to do extraordinary acts, these mundane tasks may be longed for relief. But what happens when that very relief suddenly also becomes a source of emotional trauma? What is the answer? A generic response might be therapy, but the focus of that answer must be clear to those suffering from PTSS. The conclusion that this veteran makes is that though he/she desperately doesn't want to leave his/her children again, the alternative (having another transference impact their safety) is untenable. Even in verbally asking to re-up, he/she is nonverbally signaling the opposite desire. The struggle over this decision rather than revelation of the event is the defining moment for the actor.

The first challenge with this monologue is to portray the veteran's confusion without confusing the audience. The audience must understand the difference between what is real (within the context of the story) and what is perceived. You must answer several of the common questions:

1. To whom is the subject speaking? Does that person have any connection to help? Is it a parent, a spouse, a Re-enlistment Officer, a stranger?
2. Which of the above (though not limited to those options) would make the story most compelling?
3. How recent was the incident? What is the interval between the event and the retelling of the event?
4. What will you do specifically during the "uncomfortable pause?" Several people have been credited with the saying that, "Music happens between the notes." Even though I'm giving you a book (as most are) filled with words, an actor needs to have command over the spaces between those words. Much of what you convey will be in the simplest of terms.

In Season 6 of *So You Think You Can Dance* (yes, I love dance), married couple Ryan and Ashleigh Di Lello danced together on the show for the first time during the finale. Afterwards, Director/Choreographer Adam Shankman asked, "Can I ask how that felt?" With tears streaming down her cheeks and in an inseparable embrace from her husband, she softly choked, "It was perfect." It doesn't require a lot of words to say a lot. Know what you want to communicate; it will be more than the words.

I'm Not Finished, I'm Just Stopping

Sizing canvas to make it ready for paint has always been a mystery to me. Much like priming a wall, I guess. Why can't you just throw paint on it? Would the canvas or the wall notice? I'm guessing it's because we would notice. It's one of those little gems of wisdom that the great master passes down. I imagine in some way, we all must be sized before we can be…finished.

I believe my first marriage was a case of just throwing paint on an unprepared surface. Neither one of us expected the result. We both thought the painting would be a masterpiece—something never seen before. And we were both surprised. The problem is that once you figure it out, it's tough to get all that paint off. It's easier just to throw the canvas away and start all over.

I wonder how many times that's happened? How many works of art have followed a discarded canvas? Sets a poor precedent for relationships, doesn't it? And then even when you find one that works, how do you know it's complete? How do you know you're finished?

I find myself constantly trying to tweak and perfect it. I walk away and then come back, sometimes weeks later, and see something that I think needs to be changed. Even after years, I look at my work and still find myself second-guessing my choices. Why did I use that color? I should have used a different brush. The canvas is too small. The canvas is too big. It should have been vertical. And on it goes...

And so I've come to the conclusion that I'm never really finished. I will never be completely satisfied. And so the change that I want to make isn't in the painting—it's in me. Now if you ask me if I'm finished, I will tell you no. I've just chosen this place to stop.

Notes:

This is one of my favorite pieces. Not because I think it reflects my best writing, but because it deals with a basic problem with which all writers, artists, actors, and editors struggle. When do I stop? When do I walk away? For me it's all about the process or the journey. The destination can seem somewhat disappointing. As an actor, I've never thought much of curtain calls. Quite honestly, I detest them. I would rather be backstage getting out of makeup or on my way to an after show dinner with some of the cast and crew. Conversely, I know some actors who live for the curtain call. I have no disparagement about their take. They are perfectly entitled to enjoy it.

I am simply about the work. And that's the difficult part. Unless I consciously chose to stop, I would be forever tweaking a paragraph, sentence or word. I assure you this book has been full of tweaking. Did I choose the right tweaks, I don't know. If I hadn't chosen to stop, you wouldn't be reading it because I would still be tweaking the *bejuices* out of it (be sure to put some of your own juices into it).

So given that little bit of therapy session, you may ask what are you supposed to do with it? Thank you for asking. This obviously is about the creative struggle. There is no correct answer. There is only choosing to stop. Come back in another year and your experiences will have altered your vision, even if only slightly.

There's a process for sorting information called figure and ground. Faced with an overwhelming onslaught of stimuli, we attend to some information and move other information to the background. Among other things, this process can change from moment to moment by the effect of motives and needs. What you see and want today is not necessarily what you see and want tomorrow. Therefore the story will change, the canvas will change, and the performance will change. The creative process will morph and skew and find its way back and then change again. So where do you stop? That's the important question. That's what you have to reveal to us as the piece plays out until finally we come to the place where you, the actor, have chosen to stop. I, the writer, have selected a place, but where have you, the actor, chosen yours?

It's Only a Drink

It's only a drink...

Do you know how much drinking one person has to do before it kills 'em? Because one of us, sure as hell, isn't trying hard enough.

You know what I like best about drinking? It clears the mind. Everyone thinks you're in a fog, but you're not. A fog is what you wake up in; a fog is what clears away with that first drink.

People think you're going to do something stupid when you drink. Hell, at least then I'd have an excuse. I can't explain half the stupid things I've done while I've been sober. Look at us...Oh, that's right—we both had an excuse for that.

I'm not going to lie to you; I'd rather be drinking right now, cause you'd look a whole lot better through a different pair of glasses…Just kidding.

Anyway, I don't know what all the fuss is about. It's in my genes. Everyone in my family drinks. Not everyone falls over, but I think that's a personal issue. It's all a matter of gravity—when I drink, gravity sucks.

Come on; let's get a drink. I'll be in a better frame of mind about quitting.

Notes:

One thing that makes this tricky is the challenging manner of delivery. There are distinct thoughts, which are grouped as paragraphs. However to be effective, the thoughts must be offered in a cohesive continuum otherwise it simply comes off as a stand-up routine rather than a monologue. I've seen this piece performed with a purely comedic tone and also with a melancholy foundation. Those two choices are not necessarily mutually exclusive. The rhythm however is certainly a key to its effective presentation.

1. How long has it been since your last drink? The answer to this explains your delivery within the context of the third paragraph.
2. To whom are you talking?
3. What is the relationship?
4. To what event is the speaker referring in paragraph four?
5. Is the speaker kidding in paragraph five?
6. What is the speaker quitting?

Make sure you test this one before you venture out. You may be surprised at the distance between your intent and what the audience perceives. Everyone comes with a frame of reference, so think about the possible vision that the piece may suggest.

I once did a commercial for a recovery hospital. I spoke in terms that indicated the effect on my family but never mentioned the problem. The creative director knew that the audience would impose their own issues. Sure enough, people I knew thought it was real and that I had a drinking problem, drug crisis and/or family violence issue. One person even called to ask if I was okay. I reminded them that I was an actor, but it was interesting to me who mentioned which issue. It spoke much more about them than me. Know your audience.

Jack's Adventure

What was it about Jack? I hadn't thought about him in over 40 years. In fact, if I had not stumbled across his book, I probably would have forgotten him forever. How sad considering what he had once meant to me. And yet turning the pages brought back such a good friend that I was first astounded that I remembered and then quickly amazed that I had forgotten. Perhaps it was not so much what Jack had been but rather what he had done. Not so much the happiness in his face, but more the determination in his eyes. Because to my young eyes, he had accomplished something nearly miraculous. Something that fueled my dreams and favored me with hope—Jack had built a fort...by today's standards, I'm sure that barely causes a flutter on the meter of youthful imagination. Even in my day, it wasn't long before the fort was replaced by a spaceship traversing the cosmos in search of strange new worlds. Of course one could make the case that, well that was just a fort with thrusters. And coonskin caps fell victim to glass-visored astronaut helmets. But when I opened the pages to *Jack's Adventure*, I remembered the thrill of possibilities and all the schemes to somehow duplicate his simple masterpiece. It was as though this wasn't merely a storybook, but a blueprint to "adventure." Each page brought the rush of delight as I found myself thinking, "I remember." I remembered the design and I remembered the color. I had fixed it so firmly in my imagination back then, that it seemed as though I had built the fort. In fact it seemed such a strong recollection, that I had to keep assuring myself that I hadn't actually built it. And though I am almost now tempted to have a go at it, I'll probably return to the fantasy and enjoy that as I had all those years ago. For this adventure was Jack's. And I am thankful enough just for the visit.

Notes:

I will offer that this is probably more of a tribute than

a monologue. If you wonder how much of me is in any of the other pieces, I can say without hesitation that this is *all* me. This was in fact a childhood book that I rediscovered several years ago when my elderly mother had to say goodbye to her home and independence. It was just one bittersweet moment at a time tested by the weight of goodbye.

You must decide how your character deals with this memory. Is it a time you long for or one from which you are happy to pass? That will determine how you deliver the last line. How has the character changed from the first to the last? That will establish the journey.

Since it is unlikely that you would have read about Jack, I would suggest recalling something you once owned and thinking about the emotional connection. It doesn't necessarily have to be a book, but the subject will draw something from you. Will you choose something you deeply miss, casually miss or are happy to be past it? I had forgotten Jack and don't know even in moments of deep recollection that I would have returned to that story.

There are things we would never want to forget because in the fear of forgetting we would assign great loss. And yet once it is forgotten, there is no loss, no further connection to engender any feeling. It is as though it never was.

Perhaps for the character, it is the realization that memories may eventually leave us, that tasks him. And so he begins to wonder, what else is missing? What thing or person that he thought he'd never forget, that would actually hurt to forget, doesn't because hurting would require remembrance.

Perhaps my "Jack's Adventure" is just a blueprint for what you might remember.

For me, it was and hopefully always will remain a sweet memory.

Language Barrier

No, No, wait...I need you to understand me. You have to understand *something*...Here, give me your hand. Feel this (trying to press her hand against his chest). No, it's okay. Really just feel it...My heart—do you feel that? Beating...yes...beating. That's you (pointing to her). You're doing that. You make it beat. And look—I'm breathing (taking deep breaths) See...breathing. I do that for you. I do that to see your face in the morning. And when you leave, I hold my breath until you come back. I turn blue every night. It's probably good you're not here...You're not getting any of this are you? What's the universal symbol for stupid? (Getting a laugh) Stupid?! You understand stupid? That's great you understand me. Wait a minute, that's not great, she thinks I'm stupid. No. *Not stupid*—no stupid. This is not going well...Eyes. Eyes! They're windows to the soul. Look in my eyes. Yes, right here (pointing to his eye). That's got to tell you something. Look in my eyes. That's it, look deeply...No (pulling his head back) I don't have anything in my eye…this is hopeless…Wait. Maybe you speak a second language other than English. Uhhh…amoré. That means love doesn't it? Or pizza…I can't remember which. Okay, how 'bout another language? Uhhh…Oh my god, I don't know any other languages. I am so stupid (hearing her say, "stupid"). Yes, stupid. You know "stupid." How can you not know any English except the word "stupid?" You know, if this relationship is going to work, one of us is going to have to learn a new language…okay, I guess that would be me.

Notes:

"What we have here is a failure to communicate." Such is the struggle of the character but never the actor. I state that positively because at the core of our acting objective is the need to communicate. This monologue plays to that objective twice. The monologue's character struggles to communicate his affection to the unseen character, while the actor attempts to communicate the struggle to the audience.

In this scene, you need to communicate creativity, urgency, spontaneity and frustration. If you fail at that, the lines will be meaningless. So here you need to ascertain the need for this event. Why does the main character feel compelled to express himself now? Is she leaving? Is he leaving? Is there a chance she will find someone else? Is there a threat she will find someone else?

Pay particular attention to word choice. Although the result of the situation in these last two questions may be the same, there is certainly a difference in expectations between the word "chance" and "threat." Which might be more applicable in this scenario? Why?

You might also make the scene more compelling by considering your freedom to act on a response. For instance, suppose there is safety in the fact that you can ask a question that can't be answered. If she spoke English, would you be just as willing to express yourself? That certainly would be a challenging tone to assume.

Are you single? Is she single? That might involve too much backstory, but it invests an angle that might chill the humor with the addition of a line at the end. Consider the difference if the last line read, "Okay, I guess that would be me. Your boyfriend would probably wonder why you're suddenly studying English." Or the more personal, "Okay, I guess that would be me. My brother would probably wonder why you're suddenly studying English." Either flips the piece on its end for the audience.

What begins as a sympathetic character is now a suspicious character. This is a simple reveal that functions as a twist. You have the same character as in the beginning, but the audience's affection has likely been suddenly thwarted or even betrayed. Congratulations! If you successfully communicate the emotion to that end; you have most assuredly been compelling. Use whichever ending you feel inclined. If you have different audiences, you may alternate endings to note the different responses. Break a leg!

Roses for Rosemary

Are you going to miss her?...I brought roses...She always liked roses, even when we were kids. She used to get into my mother's rose bush...She always denied it. But she had scratches everywhere. Reckless abandon. Rosemary never let anything get in her way or slow her down—least of all thorns.

Why do you think people do that? She certainly was the same way with men. When she had her eye on a guy...the rough parts didn't matter. Getting scratched—didn't matter. Of course, she went through a lot of guys finding the right one...I wonder if she ever thought she had?

She sent me something a few weeks ago. It was an old faded paper rose. I had given it to her when we were kids. I thought it might keep her out of my mom's roses. But it didn't. I thought this way she would have one that never died. But she never seemed to mind the dying...I couldn't believe she still had it after all these years.

You know, I never thought she'd live as long as she did. That's terrible, I know. It's just she took so many chances. I always thought she would die young—younger.

And here she is once again surrounded by roses.

You would have loved it, Rosemary. And this time, I'm the one with the scratches.

Notes:

When writing a monologue, I always have a particular voice and story in mind for each one. Every monologue that I've written is a sufficient piece unto itself. That is, it isn't extracted from a larger story or play. I would say that it is what it is, except that hasn't always proved to be the case. When I have assigned monologues in our Working Actor class, I initially offer very little direction. I will certainly answer specific questions if the actors choose to voice any. Most times, they do not. They simply have at it. There's something to be said for the independence and confidence that suggests, but one also has to question the logic. How many times will you have the author present to question? If your answer approaches zero, you would generally be correct.

Now I also know that people will sometimes equate questions with ignorance. In fact, that can sometimes be the nonverbal response. I can only say as I do in all of my college classes that ignorance may reside in the response but never in the question. So even if there is a mocking tone in the answer (certainly not from me, though I have been on the receiving end), have the courage to ask the question. Growth and success happens with knowledge not in fear and silence. So I am not withholding information to trap anyone, I am encouraging my students to ask questions.

Ask questions. Ask questions. Ask questions.

Ask it about acting, ask it about relationships, and ask it about life. Learn to ask questions! Without those questions, the attempt frequently goes greatly awry; however, every now and then something extraordinary happens. Someone contradicts my voice and it works. Now I say extraordinary because my voice seems completely logical and obvious to me. And though I am happy when they find my voice, I also thoroughly enjoy the walk down a different path because it reveals a certain depth to the work that further validates the writer.

What options; what breadth of experience; what explorations may lie in wait yet to be revealed? It is certainly exciting to me and I hope equally rewarding for the actor.

Consider then if you will, the various possibilities. If you are digging for gold, will you turn away the diamonds you uncover? Such discoveries could certainly await you if you are open to all possibilities.

It is because of these experiences that I sometimes lament with the actor who was told at a monologue audition, that's not what the scene is about. In those cases, I even object to the actor being told that his/her extracted monologue can only be delivered one way simply because that's the way the original piece is traditionally presented. I would rather hope that the actor failed in the delivery of his/her voice than the auditor was so narrow-minded or naive to think that a work can only reveal one meaning. We can certainly tune the voice more readily than an obdurate mindset. Possibilities are much more exciting than probabilities.

In all cases you should deconstruct the monologue. What are the clues? There's not a single successful way to present this piece, but you do need to answer the following questions. I have been fascinated by the varied answers that I've received. You won't need to guess my voice but you'll need it to make sense to you and your audience.

1. Who are you?
2. What is your relationship to Rosemary?
3. How long have you known Rosemary?
4. Has the relationship been a constant one?
5. Where is this conversation taking place?
6. What is the unusual significance of bringing roses?
7. To whom are you speaking?
8. What is that person's relationship to Rosemary?
9. The very first line is a curious question. What does it say about you?
10. What did you think about Rosemary's behavior?
11. What do you think about Rosemary's behavior of late?
12. What are you really asking by the first question in the second paragraph?
13. What has been your relationship with the opposite (or not) sex?

14. What are you really asking by the question at the end of the second paragraph?
15. What did Rosemary's return of the paper rose mean?
16. Why did you have difficulty believing that she kept it?
17. Why do you say the terrible thing at the beginning of paragraph four?
18. How old (relatively speaking) are you? This will answer whether or not this piece is appropriate for you.
19. What are the roses which surround her?
20. Aside from the literal meaning in the last line, what does it mean about you?

Yes, all of these can and must be answered by the monologue. Your job as an actor is to wring it dry so that you can give it the water of life.

You'll notice that though these questions involve Rosemary, they must reveal something about you (your character). If the monologue is not about you, then you need to make it about you or find another piece. We see *you*. We must be interested in you. Rosemary is unseen. We're not casting Rosemary; we're casting *your character*. A huge mistake some actors make is letting the monologue be about the unseen character. This monologue is not about Rosemary.

Single File

Okay, everybody line up—single file.
Let's go. One in front of the other.
And no running.
Jim, Jane—stop holding hands.
Single file everybody.
That's good Stevie. Stay behind Annie.
Jim and Bobby—stop holding hands.
Tommy, move up. Come on, keep up.
Debbie doesn't have cooties.
No, those aren't cooties.
Single file, boys and girls.
Annie. Put your dress down.
Let's go everybody. Keep moving. Keep up.
Stevie. Put Annie's dress down.
Tommy, how'd you get back here?
Sarah doesn't have cooties either.
No, those aren't cooties.
Annie where's your dress?

Bobby take Annie's dress off.

Single file. Please boys and girls.

Yes, Sammy.

As soon as we get inside Sammy, you can go to the bathroom.

Annie put your dress back on.

Jennifer, where's your other shoe?

How did it get on the roof?

Stevie!

We'll get it back. Just take your time and don't step on anything sharp…

Okay just sit there and I'll come back and carry you to the nurse and get the splinter out.

Stevie!!

What Sammy?

Yes, that is cold when that happens. All right, we'll stop at the office and you can call your mother.

Okay, your grandmother.

Don't worry, we'll find somebody.

Single file everybody. I'm not going to say it again.

Walk! Do not run!

Annie, I thought I told you to put your dress back on.

Well who has it now?

Stevie!!!

Okay Annie, sit over there with Jennifer.

Sammy, I know it's cold, but I told you we were going inside.

Fine. Sit over there with Jennifer and Annie.

No Jennifer, Sammy doesn't have cooties. That's just…never mind.

Just sit quietly.

Sammy! Don't take your pants off!

I don't care how cold it is.

Jim, Jane, Bobby! Stop holding hands.

Single file! What did I just say?

Has anybody seen Stevie?

Stevie! How did you get up there?!

Okay, step back, sit down and don't move. I'm coming right up.

Class, listen to me. We're going inside—quickly.

Everybody behind you—has cooties. Run!

Notes:

Some (okay, many) years ago just after high school, I worked part-time as a substitute teacher at my old elementary school. Seeing the classroom from the opposite angle allowed me to learn the first key to education is control, so turn off that mp3 player and cell phone and pay attention to what you're reading. There's no such thing as multitasking (look it up).

Back to the task, I didn't base this monologue on that experience but on my earlier experience staying in line as a student in elementary school. It was very important at that time to have recess and burn off that energy so we would be more controllable. I know that exercise also helps the brain to function better. During the fall and spring when the weather was temperate but too wet for playground activity, we would line up and walk around the parking lot. We did get to talk but there was something penal about the exercise. One day, someone with more sardonic movie experience than I had, started to whistle the prisoners' march from *The Bridge on the River Kwai*. It was genius beyond my understanding, and soon many of us joined in. We marched and whistled with great enjoyment. Our enthusiasm was not shared by the monitors and we were soon relegated to silent walking. I believe there was a rights violation somewhere—the right to organize and whistle. Well, at least it sounds familiar. Nevertheless our silencing began the growth of an anti-establishment rebellion in us. Rock on. Down with the Man (although these were mostly female teachers). Oh, wait a minute; I'm also a college instructor now. Maybe a little control isn't so bad.

I have essentially formatted this monologue in single file to correspond to the scenario. It is a series of thoughts, problems, distractions and characters. The challenge for you will be distinctly placing the characters and the issues that focus eyelines on their wardrobe, positions and locations. You will also find the task in having your attention continually shift, based on new and increasingly problematic trials.

If the term cooties is too passé, simply replace it with any other imaginary nemesis from your childhood.

The build should be slow, which requires many steps, but don't expect to place a step with each line. Grouping the elements will work nicely. Most importantly, have fun with this monologue. That's not to say that you shouldn't with the other humorous monologues, it's just this scenario can reflect an experience shared by most of the audience. These are elements we've all experienced either as children, teachers, parents or siblings. Everyone should enjoy the walk; but no whistling.

Sitting Down

Now I stood here and you sat right there and told me. I know, cause I heard it. You asked me. You said, "Missy, can your folk use anything new at the store?" Was there anything we wanted; anything we needed? And I told you. I stood right here and I told you. Now I didn't ask for nothing, cause I thought in the having it, that would be good enough. But you said if my folk bought it from the store, you'd see to it that I got a share. I know, cause I heard it. You said, "Missy, I'm gonna treat you right cause you is a big help." That's what you said, Mr. Sims. You said that right here. Then when you told me you got it, I felt good. I felt *real* good. Not cause of the share but cause I did something good and it was gonna help folk. And I thought you is a good man, Mr. Sims. Praise be for Mr. Sims, cause he help folk. Then I asked you some time later how it was and you said, "Missy, nobody is buying it so there ain't gonna be no share," and I was sad, real sad, not for the share but cause I was sure folk could use it. So I said I was sorry that you had gone to all that trouble for me. I felt bad, real bad Mr. Sims, causing you all that trouble.

Then when Percy got sick and couldn't go to the store like he usually does, I went down myself and thought I would buy some to make amends. I didn't need that much but I didn't want you hurt for something I said is good. But when I got there, I couldn't find any, so I asked that young man where it was and he said you is sold out. He said it sold out in one week and you is waiting for another order, it was so good. Now that's not what you told me, Mr. Sims, so I figured they didn't tell you. But I knew you'd want to know, so I come for my share, just like you said so. I wouldn't have asked for it and I wouldn't have expected it but you said I would get a share and I come for it. I know you didn't mean to tell me that, but Missy has always been good to you and you said so right here. I know; I heard it. You was sitting right in that chair leaning on your desk the way you do and Missy was standing right here. Now I'm all caught up on my chores and I'm not cheatin' you outta any time, so I will just sit here (Missy sits) and wait for my share like you said. And I will thank you for it, Mr. Sims. Missy will truly thank you for it.

Notes:

There's much to be considered with this monologue. Let's begin with the three names. First, I offer my apologies to those who are affectionately known as Missy. In this story, the name is used as a personal generic. That is, it identifies a particular woman but could easily refer to any female in that position and time (first half of the 20th century). It operates as a pretense for affection by someone who nevertheless wishes to maintain a distance.

Mr. Sims wishes to suggest a close relationship, while maintaining one that offers some respectable detachment. "Percy," on the other hand, is a more conventional name. Though I am somewhat reluctant to use the term "conventional," it would be more traditionally a common name rather than a nickname. The difference could be used to imply a gender distinction or station. Though perhaps too subtle to be noticeable by anyone except the reader of these notes, Sims has been chosen due to its close proximity to the word "sins." Regardless of the audience notice, you as the actor can use this information to understand the basis for Missy's actions. Knowing these things allows Missy to be presented not as someone naïve, but rather someone who is evidently smarter than Sims would consider.

Had Percy not fallen ill, Missy would not have made the trip to the store to learn of Sims' deception. Once she does, she states her case in a well-devised manner. She doesn't accuse Sims of lying. Such an accusation, regardless how truthful, would likely lead to her dismissal. Instead of that tack, she offers Sims an out. She suggests that he was misinformed. That proposal allows him to save face and pay Missy her due; however Missy isn't in it for the money. She never was. She simply wanted to help her employer and help those (folk) of similar station. Then you might ask, why request her share? If that's all she wanted, why not dismiss the information with the knowledge that she was correct and her folk were being helped?

The payment serves a different purpose. It validates Missy and warns Sims not to underestimate her worth. The revelation of this purpose doesn't really happen in the lines but rather in an action. Missy has noted that she stood in her employer's presence. He sat and she stood. However in waiting for the payment, she sits. That action says as much about Missy as anything else in the monologue. That action should not be self-indulgent, but it should be unequivocal.

One other thing to note is the shift between the first

person "I" and third person "Missy." This situation could easily come down to a he said, she said argument; however Missy serves as her own witness. There is the Missy who presents her case as a first person principal of the verbal contract and the Missy who serves as a witness to both parties of the agreement. She uses this to reaffirm the correctness of her memory and the unwritten contract. She is at once both party to and witness of the agreement. In all of her simplicity, Missy is a wonderfully astute character. Enjoy her growth and victory.

Slating

My name is _____ and I'll be doing "Furthermore" from A.R. Gurney's *Last Will and Testament*. I'll be reading from pages 68 and 69. Beginning with paragraph three on page 68 and continuing through paragraph seven, which is really the first paragraph on page 69…Actually, I'll be starting half way through paragraph three. But I will go to the end of paragraph seven, which again, is paragraph one, depending upon how you look at it. Also those page numbers are from the hardback edition. I don't know what page it is in the soft cover version because I don't have that copy. It could even all be on one page in that form. I just don't know. Maybe if someone has that copy, they could share it with us. During the break or something.

Also, I'll be doing this with an English accent from Barnaby Street — Not the one in London, but the one in Southwark...east side...between the 400 and 700 block...during the 1950s...in the Irish pubs.

And most of the material will be verbatim. Except those words I couldn't understand, so I just left those out. I really don't think it changes much of the meaning. There are so many other words; I think that you'll get the gist of it. But if you have any questions, I brought the book with me and you can ask me afterwards. I'll be hanging around outside to see how I did.

Oh—and I would have done a longer piece, but Amazon.com screwed up my order and I just got the book this morning. So please bear with me.

Anyway here it is—*almost* word for word. You can start the time now. And Furthermore...

Notes:

The source for this was a longer than normal slate in our Working Actor 1 class. I simply expanded on what was otherwise a curious experience. Since many monologue auditions have a time limit, I wondered what would happen if you spent your entire allotment slating? Ordinarily, you would state your name, the title of the piece or title of the original work from which it is taken and the author's name. That's typically outside of the time limit as it would begin with the first word or action of the piece.

I've often wondered how long someone could fool the timer with this monologue. Of course it would be a one and done. The first time it finds its way into a large format audition, the curtain would be pulled back to expose the real wizard. Still it's worth an exploration since at least elements of this do raise some bewildered curious eyebrows.

The real test here is not to play everything on the same note. There's a certain "oh yeah, and I have to tell you," pattern that could easily give it away too early. And therein lies the real test. How long can you keep the absurdity going? If you essentially begin each paragraph with an implied, "Oh yeah," you'll be finished before you end.

Many of my monologues create a difficult challenge. Finding the character is essential but not the lone task. You have to create a scene. So contrary to my general instruction to play the scene appropriately to the unseen character on stage, this one *is* played out to the entire audience. After all, technically it is the slate. For those auditors who love to have the actor look at them—enjoy.

As you begin the piece, be careful not to accurately slate. The false slate has to come at the beginning as written. In this case, you can't ascribe the work to me by title and name. And incidentally, there is no piece by Gurney entitled *Last Will and Testament* aside from the one which may be privy to his attorney.

There is one line I've written that may be chilling to most auditors, at least the ones I know. "I'll be hanging around outside to see how I did." Is there a back door? The alternate exit can avoid much of the Simon Cowell honesty, unless of course you *can* handle the truth.

The reference to the English accent is actually my response to a stage director, who for an audition asked me to use my "best" British accent. My first impulse was to say, "You mean instead of that crappy one I usually choose?" Okay, I didn't say that. I didn't say "crappy." The ridiculous nature of that request is evidenced by the scores of British accents that actually exist. How about picking one you deem appropriate and I'll have a go at it. I mentioned this to a fellow actor who once played at the British Embassy in Washington D.C. After his forage into the accent, he said that every Brit he met afterwards gave him a different twist on the tongue. I guess he wasn't using his "best"- accent.

The note about a book being delivered that same day did surface in the student's slate. So let me repeat a rule—never apologize. This rule applies specifically to the audition scenario. Don't set yourself up for failure or believe that will assuage the note of mediocrity. The surprise may be that you did well, until you tempered our consideration with the idea that you probably didn't.

Gary Wheeler

Someday When You Dream About Me

Someday when you dream about me—and you will...you'll wake up frightened. Not that anything terrible has happened, but frightened that you might be feeling something—something that you haven't admitted to. Something you weren't aware of. Something you've hidden from your consciousness, which only your inner self is willing to accept—me. Oh, you'll deny it and shake it off as the result of some midnight snack, but the uneasiness will linger. And then it'll drift away as you go about your day. Fading, you hope, into just another crazy dream. But just when you thought it was gone; just when you thought it was forgotten, someone will say something and suddenly, inexplicably—the dream will rush back. And there it starts all over again. Except it's not so inexplicable. It's just me—and it's completely understandable—and frightening. Because you know what the explanation is. You've allowed yourself to wonder. However briefly, however carelessly, you couldn't *not* think about me—and wonder. Go ahead and deny it…Laugh about it…Cry if you want to. But we both know, it'll happen. Maybe not tonight or tomorrow night. But it *will happen*. And I'll know it. I'll know it when you look at me and look away with that "I hope he doesn't know it," look. And then I'll smile and you'll know I know.

Keep dreaming sweetheart…I'll be there eventually. (optional ending)

Notes:

Dreams are always an interesting source of material. Logic and sense seem greatly skewed. I've had wonderful ideas for movies in my dreams. And somehow knowing that I'm dreaming, I tell myself I have to remember this when I wake up. However, when I wake up and do remember it, I think that it makes no sense at all (Note "The Sense of it All" later in the book).

Over the years, I've also been amazed not at the people I dream about, but rather the people I don't. People I've thought would play or have played a significant role in my life, never appear. And then there are the occasional "visits" from people whom I have no recollection of ever meeting or even seeing anywhere. I would imagine they assume a personality of my choosing and at the end of the dream, I am sad to see them go. They never return. Then there are some special people from long past who turn up semi-regularly to work through what was never resolved (at least in my mind). Dreams can be a source of comfort or discomfort, but always a source of material (however crazy it seems).

This monologue is not about a dream. Then why, do you ask, did I mention all of the above? Because this character has an understanding of or at least a belief about dreams and the power they can have over the conscious world. You have to decide if your interpretation will work for the character or if you need to assign a different view.

At first reading, you'll probably conclude that this is a very haughty or at least self-assured individual. And that may be as far as you take it. That would certainly be a logical approach. Is this then just a final slap—a chance to get in one last dig, having been kicked to the curb? If so, that will certainly offer an unsettling portrayal for the audience. They will not approve of the character and that may be exactly your intent. There has to be an antagonist.

What other options might you have for this character? Well, this individual may not be as haughty as he/she might be damaged. Suppose this isn't a motive of revenge as it is a desperate suggestion of hope. He/she might be trying to impose a dream upon the other that will eventually lead him/her back. We might not view that as a healthy choice in reality, but in drama it certainly could prove an interesting choice.

In that situation, it's not just the actor who is portraying a character, but also the character that is portraying a desperate persona.

Nothing is typically so cut and dry, that you can't find a different take on it and perhaps a more interesting and uncommon take. If the material is excised from a published and performed work, you will undoubtedly hear that it comes with expectations. That is somewhat of a sad and narrow-minded view held by that particular audience. Great minds explore. But be prepared to hit the wall on occasion. Just like in dreams, not everything or everyone makes sense.

The Confession

In the name of the Father and of the Son and of the Holy Spirit, Amen. Bless me Father for I have sinned. It has been three months since my last confession.

Well, I've been kind of busy.

Doing what I came here to talk to you about.

No, I couldn't get here any sooner. I was doing it out of town.

Well they didn't have one there. Anyway, isn't it more important that I came here as soon as I got back home?

I flew. I didn't pass any churches on the way.

I thought this was confession. I didn't know I'd have to explain myself.

Father, there are people waiting.

They're not here to see me. They're here for confession.

I don't know what they did…I don't even remember what I did now.

Okay, why I don't I start over. In the Name of the Father and of the Son and of the Holy Spirit, Amen. Bless me Father for I have sinned. It has been—two minutes since my last confession.

Thank you, Father. I make it a point to come as often as I can.

Notes:

I'll begin with apologies to my Catholic readers. Confession is good for the soul; it's also not too bad for humor.

This monologue probably comes from a multitude of sources and experiences though I have no recollection of any personal dialogue that inspired this piece. Perhaps there was divine intervention, but I wrote it anyway.

I've always enjoyed this challenge of delivery. It's as though I've written a scene and then excised one character's dialogue. Truth is, if you were to write out the lines, it's not as funny. This format keeps the audience engaged and has been used successfully by several comediennes over the years. We get the answer and have to jump back and form the question, then jump ahead to hear the next answer and back to form the question and so on. It requires the audience to maintain a critical ear.

Make sure you hear the question and allow a reasonable time for the unheard dialogue to occur. You can cheat on that somewhat to keep a workable pace, but too short a period and the audience won't buy it nor have the time to connect with you and the scene.

As in many cases, one of the crucial choices you have to make is how to begin. It's not about the words; it's about the attitude. Are you reverential or matter-of-fact? How would that difference affect your delivery choices throughout the rest of the monologue?

Any material dealing with religion is a tricky subject. This is particularly true when you don't know the makeup of the audience. Do you consider a broad base of beliefs or ignore everyone's persuasion?

Other questions include:
1. What were you doing out of town that you now need confessing?
2. Does it matter?
3. What is your tone with the priest?

You'll need to establish the physical arrangement of

the confessional for the audience. Consider your position within the confessional when positioning yourself to the audience. The priest will be positioned so that his ear is favoring your face. There is only one doorway or curtain for entrance and exit. The reference to the other people will favor that direction.

Finally are you leaving us with the idea that you'll confess everything regardless or that essentially you've fooled the priest without really confessing anything? That choice will reveal the most about your character. That information isn't in the line; that will be what you bring to the confessional.

Gary Wheeler

The Happy Little Girl

Yes, I understand. Everybody keeps telling me that, but I think I should be able to cry. Doesn't anybody understand that? I know what I'm supposed to do...I know what's expected. But I'm tired of everyone telling me that...I understand that. My life is supposed to be exactly what my daddy expects it be. Why is that? Why can't tomorrow be different? Why can't I be different? I stand in the laundry room folding his clothes and think, "There's got to be more to life than this." Is it wrong to think that? Am I a bad person because I don't want to fold clothes?...These hurt.

My daddy said I should be happy. I should take my medication. He got mad when I didn't...See, I stopped taking it a few days ago and now I've broken one of my favorite things. That's it on the floor. It was a little glass girl. My daddy gave it to me when I was 10. He said it was called the "Happy Little Girl" and should remind me of what I should be. He told me I should always look at it when I wanted to cry…I don't think I can fix it. But it's okay. I don't cry anymore…but I think I should…It's okay to cry isn't it? I used to cry.

I just got tired of feeling this way…feeling sorta…nothing. Not especially good, but not bad either. I shouldn't have to feel nothing afterwards, should I? I shouldn't have to do that if I don't want to. But nobody believes me cause he's real careful…Is he going to wake up? He's not going to like that I broke it. He's not gonna like it at all. I have to clean it up. He's going to see it lying there when he wakes up.

Maybe we can find another one before he wakes up. Can you take these off please? They hurt. My daddy says nothing's gonna hurt. So that's what I told him when I broke the happy little girl …I think I should cry now. This would be a good time to cry, wouldn't it? Can you help me? I think I should cry now.

Notes:

For any of these monologues, it may be helpful to rewrite them and organize the spacing as it lends to your portrayal. As I've mentioned, some of these monologues are formatted as one long paragraph. They shouldn't be presented that way. Even with paragraphs, as in this case, place your thoughts and pauses to punctuate your choices. Failing to do so, will certainly affect your performance.

You always need to know where you wind up, in order to determine how you should start. In this case, the last paragraph will indicate your condition at the beginning. Your audience will be able to reflect at the conclusion that your beginning state was logical and appropriate. Those two conditions do not necessarily go hand-in-hand.

Herein is the tale of a troubled young woman. How young will depend upon you and the reasonable expectations of the audience. I want you to be aware of your apparent age. That to some extent will be affected by the distance you play from your audience. Some people look older than their years. Check your hands.

I've always been in that category until lately when I've started to catch up. I try to mitigate that by standing next to older people. When my mother turned 97, I asked if she knew how old she was. When I told her, she said she didn't know she was that old. I asked her how old she thought she was and she replied only 91. Much can be said about your vantage point. Your vantage point needs to be the mirror. A younger director may cast you older and an older director may cast you younger. Somewhere in there, you shouldn't believe either, but take the work. Believe your mirror and not your headshot. There are plenty of headshots out there that are laughable.

All of that to say, don't make the audience dismiss the

scenario because of how young or old you really look. Take a poll, but don't ask your friends unless they are true and brutally honest friends.

This monologue, if I may, is an interesting exercise in our understanding of emotional expression. Initially, most of my students would casually describe this woman as unemotional. We describe someone who screams or cries as being highly emotional. The behavior is demonstrable. And yet this young woman has a hurricane of emotion that's fighting to get out. That can be a compelling struggle if you are able to express what's been thwarted by medication. It's not a lack of emotion but rather a challenging expression of emotion artificially constrained. I would be much more impressed by someone who can deliver this rather than someone who can tritely scream and shout.

This process may also require some further investigation into the submersion of emotion. We have many examples, in our lives and elsewhere, regarding emotional expression. The examples that are needed for this piece are often locked away from our common view.

You will need to answer what her father was "real careful" about. That will need to be clear to the audience.

Determine your objective for the audience and be specific about the choices that will deliver the intended result.

The Right Words

Hello, I'm Dr. Harbison. I'm afraid I have some bad news. It doesn't look like he's going to make it.

(to oneself) Too presumptuous—suppose it's not bad news?

Hi. Dr. Harbison. Have you thought about what you're going to do after he's gone? Well start thinking.

(to oneself) Too presentational—sounds like an infomercial.

Do you remember that old expression about "kicking the bucket?" Well right now, he's in there kickin' it.

(to oneself) Too metaphorical—she might miss the point.

Would you like to see him before he dies? Well don't

stop for coffee on the way to his room.

(to oneself) Too obtuse—suppose she doesn't drink coffee. (composing oneself) Okay, I've got to take my time and find the right words. (sarcastically) Don't want another bad bedside manner review.

(responding to a cell phone) Harbison...oh.

Harbison completes the call and returns to rehearsing.

Hello, I'm Dr. Harbison. I just wanted to prepare you so that you wouldn't be alarmed when you went in to see him—we put toe tags on all of our patients.

(to oneself) Too unbelievable. Besides the zippered bag will probably tip her off.

(big overly warm consoling smile) Hi. I'm Dr. Harbison...

Notes:

I should begin this by confessing that I've never known a doctor with a bad bedside manner. There have been a few who could stand to warm up a little, but for the most part, they've been compassionate and attentive physicians. I also realize that now that I've stated that, one is looming; so this one's for you, Bud.

This is obviously an intrapersonal conversation. To some extent, it's the same exercise we take when rehearsing for an audition. We say the line and second guess. We say the line and guess again. Hopefully we arrive at the correct delivery beforehand. In this case, it's too late.

Response to the darkness of this humor will differ from audience to audience depending upon how quickly the actor will make it safe for the audience to laugh. With such material, your audience must ask themselves if they should laugh. In some manner, you have to let them know that it's okay to laugh about it. Unless of course you are reading this now and thinking, "This is supposed to be funny?"

I have to admit, I've seen it done without a single laugh. At which point I want to say, "Give me that script." Now the danger with helping a script is that you can actually drain the humor from it. I've had actors try to "help" scenes that they already thought were funny. They wanted to make it funnier. The character was somewhat amusing but the scene was subsequently flat. If you allow the humor to breathe, we'll generally enjoy the breath and perhaps not be able to catch ours. If you think the humor needs resuscitation, it will likely get swallowed in your mouth-to-mouth efforts.

As you prepare each delivery attempt, remember that you (Dr. Harbison) are searching for the correct tone. Each attempt should therefore be somewhat different from the others. In fact there is some help in that, as after each attempt Harbison complains about how it fails. Incorporate that judgment in the delivery. This is likely one of the few monologues with directions embedded in the script.

Let me offer a caution about props. There is a direction in this monologue that calls for a cell phone. Today almost all of us carry a cell phone. We don't really have to feign one.

Ordinarily I would avoid the use of props in an audition. I say that even though I've used them myself. The problem lies in their comfortable use. Given that you would have rehearsed this, I think the use of a prop is acceptable. We view our entertainment with the willing suspension of disbelief. We are willing to suspend as long as you don't thwart our willingness. In this case, the extended digits (thumb and little finger) representing a phone will no doubt bring us out of the scene, so use your cell, but practice it. (I've just recently read that a company has developed a phone glove, which *would* allow us to use our finger and thumb to make calls). The problem with using props without serious rehearsal is that they will either be fumbled or telegraphed. (Is there anyone besides me who knows what a telegraph is?) We'll see you prepare to use the prop just before the prop is scripted to be used, and we're out of the moment.

Know that where the suspension drops is different for different people. Someone once told me where they dropped out of the movie *Men in Black*. He said it is too unbelievable when the car turns upside down and drives along the ceiling in the tunnel. So, I asked, about the previous scenes with the various aliens and the flash pen that makes you forget everything. Is all of that believable? I think he said, "What flash pen?" He was obviously watching too closely. This reminds me, I think I've forgotten my point.

Oh yes, if you can't effectively rehearse that prop,

don't use it. And even then be careful. No one is casting you because you used a prop or not casting you because you didn't. Always remember this statement where X is the variable. Not much of an actor, but he/she sure can X. In this case, X would equal "use a prop." Substitute X for just about anything except "act."

The Sense of it All

Just before I woke up this morning, I was having the most wonderful dream. You weren't in it…I dreamt that I was running through this field of wildflowers. It must have been late spring. I remember that it seemed warm, but not uncomfortably so. It was probably mid-May – you know, just before it starts to get humid…I don't remember having clothes on, but I may have…Whether I did or didn't doesn't mean anything. But I think the ambivalence is important. Not wearing clothes right now would make a big difference…Isn't that one of the great things about dreams – the freedom to experience something without consequences. You can't do that awake. Everything has consequences. What I eat this morning is going to have consequences later. What I ate last night already did. Life is all about limits. Not dreams – no limits, no guilt…Anyway I'm in this field of wildflowers and it's nice and warm. Then suddenly I notice this one flower that's making some kind of

…sound. I stop to listen and realize that it's singing. But what is it singing? I know the song, but can't quite place it. So I get a little closer and try to listen harder. What are the words? What are the words?! And then I hear them. It's singing, "Where Have All the Flowers Gone?" And I think, well that's a stupid song to sing. Now the fact that a flower is singing doesn't strike me as odd. I'm judging its repertoire. Isn't that great about dreams? There's some perverted sense of normalcy that only applies to that specific dream…So anyway, I'm listening to this flower, thinking why are you singing that song, when I look up and notice that all of the other flowers *are* gone. There's nothing around me anywhere but grass. So the song makes sense after all. And I'm left with this wonderfully contented feeling. You can't say that about life. If a flower suddenly started singing right now, we'd all be wondering how is that possible, instead of listening to the words. Are you listening to the words? Does any of this make sense? Then you must be awake.

Notes:

This is one of the monologues we typically assign on the first night of our Working Actor 1 class. I can tell by the third sentence ("You weren't in it") whether or not the student is on track. Just by the delivery and timing of that one line, I know:

1. The relationship.
2. If you are retelling an event or experiencing it for the first time.
3. If the other person responded or you're simply reading a line.
4. What the dream means to you.

Now by timing, I mean to include the time between the second and third sentence. You'll notice that an ellipsis follows the third sentence but only a period concludes the second. In monologues the lack of other punctuation does not necessarily mean a continuation of thought without pause. You have the words on the page. As an actor, you have to give them life. Aside from what the writer may have supplied, you have to either connect or otherwise break the dots. Now that being said, do pay some attention to the punctuation. In detective work, we call that a clue. I have seen some actors completely ignore punctuation. That's generally too much license.

Another line that gives some glimpse into your understanding is, "And I think, well that's a stupid song to sing." If you are reading this for the first time or as a first time experience, you will emphasize "stupid song." If however, you are remembering and thus retelling the dream, you will emphasize, "And I think." Because as you read further, you will discover that you had already come to the conclusion that it made sense. The subtle distinctions will challenge and prove your understanding.

Now this is a longer piece and probably too long for most audition scenarios, but it is a good exercise. I've seen this delivered in 2+ minutes and 4+ minutes.

Pacing yourself is an important choice. You have to set the pace for the unseen character and thus the audience to stay with you. If it's too fast, they will have no idea what you're attempting to accomplish other than finish. If it's too slow, it sounds very self-indulgent. I've heard both.

The other things to consider in your pacing are the tangential thoughts. You describe the dream and then the significance of each element before going back to retelling the dream again. That gives you a wonderful opportunity to create a rhythm. Without that variety, the piece will seem to play on one note. With too much variety most responses will be as Emperor Joseph II supposedly said to Mozart, "There are simply too many notes." I trust you get the meaning.

A side note, about which I have some conflict, is singing the song verse included. For those unfamiliar with the piece, "Where Have All the Flowers Gone," is a song by Pete Seeger sung by Peter, Paul and Mary. You are not obliged to sing those words in the monologue. Most do. Some even know the tune. If you don't know the song and attempt another melody for an audience that does know the song, it will clunk. This is a good reason to either research, or as I continually harp on, to ask questions. You don't need to have a wonderful voice to attempt the song, but attempting the song correctly, may add a wonderful voice.

This monologue also flagged another myth in class. After the presentations in the second class, I would ask each student how much time they spent on preparing and rehearsing the piece. The only instruction that was given was don't memorize it. One student told me that he/she hadn't looked at it during the week, because they wanted it to be "fresh." I advised them that their performance *wasn't* fresh; it was raw because they didn't understand the monologue. Fresh is something an actor brings to every take and every performance. That can't happen unless you prepare. "An actor prepares," (Stanislavski).

Thinking Ahead

So, he says to me I need tie rod ends. Tie rod ends?! I says. Whadda ya think I am? You think I'm some ____? You think I just fell off a truck? You think I don't know what you're doing? I come in here for struts and you're tryin' to jack up the price on me? So he shows me...and whadda ya know, I need tie rod ends. No _____ kiddin. Whole thing winds up costin' me four hundred bucks. Hey, whadda ya gonna do? Sometimes you gotta hurt a little now to keep from hurtin' more later. You know what mean? I'm just saying. I coulda been riding down the road with my new struts and BAM! My tires fall off. It's all about thinking ahead. That's what separates us from the animals. We think ahead. Cause if you don't think ahead Charlie, you might as well be roaming the streets with those other strays. You know what mean? Always looking around. Never sure where your next meal is. Hoping you don't get hit, though that would probably be a blessing for a miserable son of a bitch. But lucky for you Charlie, you don't have to worry about that no more. You know what I mean?

Car rides pretty good now, dudinit, Charlie? I mean you'd have to have that blindfold off to tell this was a dirt road.

You got insurance, Charlie?

I can't take the gag out, just shake your head.

That's too bad; you shoulda thought ahead, Charlie. I'm just saying. Separates us from the animals.

Notes:

Fill in the blanks according to your comfort level.

Along time ago, I was in this business—not the "mechanic" business but the auto mechanic and tire business. The general manager complained that the service ticket per car wasn't high enough. He instructed me that if a car came in for an oil change, you should be able to find $200 worth of additional work. All cars need work; you just have to look. It is amazing the number of cars on the road that at any given moment should have some preventative maintenance that really does ultimately save money, but the "push" never sat well with me. I also learned that people will often make the comfortable decision rather than the correct one. Long since out of that business, I am now on the other end. If my car needs servicing, it's always at least $400. If I need an oil change, I know it's going to cost $400. That's why even today, I change my own oil. Yesterday (as of this writing) I was changing the brake pads on my car (if you are reading this book that means the car still stops). So in regards to the beginning scene, I have been on both ends.

The character came from writing a piece for a

Working Actor student. That's not to say I imagined this individual as a hit man. In fact, I would not imagine him as such. If I wanted to be obvious, I would cast a guy like the one I once saw walk into that cell phone store. If from the outset of the story, you wanted people to look at a guy and think, he's a killer—this was your man. It would be something you would need to determine that serves the story. If you don't want the audience to know, you can't cast that guy. If you cast him as a doctor, people would think he was a doctor who killed people. He really did have a great face for it. And I hope if he ever reads this book, he doesn't know I'm referring to him.

That instance aside, some casting gives away the story from the beginning. You may see a group of minor, almost cameo, roles filled by unknowns and one prominent actor. Guess who did it? There has to be a balance between what the name will bring to the box office and effective storytelling. I vote for effective storytelling and let that carry the box office.

So for this student, I wrote something that wouldn't be given away at the beginning by his type but could be perceived in retrospect as plausible. If we had started with the piece rather than the actor, then that design would have necessitated effective casting.

You have some physical business to lock down. You are in a car. Make sure to place and keep Charlie to your right, unless of course you are playing this over the pond. Now the question becomes how adept are you at suggesting the steering wheel without it becoming the focal point of the scene? If you suggest it, it needs to be recognized and dismissed almost immediately by the audience. This scene isn't about you driving a car. Don't overplay the business. Keep the movements subtle. When it's over, you don't want the audience thinking that you were a lousy driver as the car was undoubtedly all over the road. A good rule of thumb is to establish and diminish.

As always, the language has to work for you. If its

color is not suitable for you, that doesn't mean you can't smooth those corners and still present a compelling piece. You may certainly use the slang and expressions from your corner of the world. By that I mean, don't put it on as much as let it come out. The piece will feel more honest and the audience won't be interrupted in their experience by the clunking nature of a monologue out of tune with you.

Gary Wheeler

Two Kinds of Men

There are only two kinds of men in this world—good ones and bad ones. The good ones are never bad enough and the bad ones…break your heart. Take Roger, for instance. He was very bad. Just the thought of him would make my momma shudder. But I know someone in her past did the same thing to her momma. And when they shudder, that makes us want them even more. That was why I wanted Roger. That and the fact that he would look at me like I was the last cool drop of water on a blistering July afternoon. Of course I wanted respect and courtesy, but I wanted to be that water too. I wanted to be that last drop of something to somebody who burned hotter than that July sun. And I found that in Roger. And my momma knew it. She warned me that he would never change and I told her that I didn't want him to. And she said someday I would. But I wouldn't listen. Roger wanted me so bad and I wanted him to want me that way. So I gave him that drink...I guess what I forgot was that it never stays July. Oh, I could see the change. It wasn't overnight, but looking back it sure seemed like it. My momma never said I told you so. I think that was because her momma did and she remembered how much that hurt. She told me someday I'd find a good man...if I was open to one. And I was. And that's what I found. Momma even said, "This one is a good find." And I know she's right...On those hot July afternoons, I bring him a drink and he seems content...In a few more years our daughter will be that age and I suppose I'll be the one telling her that there are only two kinds of men in the world. And I will try not to shudder.

Notes:

With acknowledgement to Twain, Faulkner, Fitzgerald and Quiller-Couch, someone wrote that you need to be willing to "kill your darlings." I also emphasize this in my video production courses and

Spielberg essentially states this approach in his interview on editing *Jaws*. Despite how much you love the word, frame, sentence, sequence, scene, or chapter, if it doesn't serve the story or rhythm, or otherwise impedes the progress, "kill your darlings." If revenge is a dish best served cold, then editing is the ice.

I note that to say, of all the monologues in this book, this one is my darling. It didn't start out that way. I don't expect each new one to be my favorite, though that would definitely be an encouragement to keep writing, especially when the muses come and go. I think what elevated this monologue in my own expectations was the first actress to perform it. After spending some time working on it, she stated her struggle coming to grips with the piece, as it resonated with her own experiences. In essence, she said it hit home too hard.

So there I stood on common ground with this young

African-American woman. It was a wonderful experience for me to watch her performance and know that despite the physical differences of our age, gender and race, we both understood this character. There is a commonality in our humanity that crosses all barriers and in so doing, brings us together. It is as though the barrier only exists in expectation; you see it ahead but once you cross it and turn around, you realize it was never there. Such is the wonderful experience of art.

This monologue comes out of the notion that females are attracted to bad boys and that their mothers have a bad boy alarm, because they too were attracted to bad boys. And we all know about bad boys.

There is one significant omission in this monologue that indicates where she is in this struggle. Can you name it? What does the omission mean?

Begin your preparation by answering these questions:

1. To whom are you speaking?
2. Where does this conversation take place?
3. What precipitated this conversation?
4. Why are you telling this story?

Given your specific answers to the above questions, I also want you to consider how you will choose to end the monologue. You have the last line. What will you do with it? As the world doesn't begin with the first word, it also doesn't end with the last. What would happen next?

And please don't say, "Scene," to conclude your performance. I'm throwing down the gauntlet. That is a terribly disruptive force to the experience. Only a director should call, "Action" and "Cut!" The auditor or casting director should call, "Scene." The actor should just finish and move gently out of the scene.

Think about it. There's nothing more jarring then to

watch a tender performance and have the actor break character and the fourth wall by suddenly calling, "Scene." As if we're too dense to figure out that's the end. Stop it, I say! I'm shouting from the rooftop. Stop the insanity! That was never meant for the actor. And if you're giving monologue instruction, stop telling them to do it. Can you imagine the artist who upon finishing the canvas cries "Painting!" (I think I have another monologue brewing) Let's just enjoy the scene and not shatter it.

When I Told Her

We were on the way to meet friends for dinner when I told her. She was staring out the window and I quietly said that I had had an affair. I didn't tell her with whom or how long it lasted or even when it ended. And she never asked. In fact, she didn't say anything. She just kept staring out the window. For a second, I wasn't sure that she had heard me or that I had even told her. I started to wonder if I was still practicing in my head and hadn't actually said anything. But I had. I can recognize my voice when it comes out of my mouth…and still she never looked at me. She didn't say anything the entire way to the restaurant. That's the kind of silence people mean when they say, "It's deafening." I couldn't even hear the traffic for the quiet in the car…When we arrived at the restaurant, she greeted our friends with a warm smile. We exchanged hugs and kisses with them and sat down at the table as if it had been any other dinner…We got through drinks and appetizers and salads and I was halfway through my beef tenderloin when it happened. She started to cry. Not my wife—our friend's wife. It wasn't out right sobbing at first, just the struggle as she tried not to cry. But somehow she was still able to choke out, "I know about you." I was politely looking away when she said it, but I think I spasmed at the indictment. I felt trapped; she knows about me. But then I felt strangely defensive. How the hell can she know about me? How dare she accuse me. Here. Now I was afraid to look at my wife. Here's the scene I expected in the car and now it would play out in a crowded restaurant. Now there would be witnesses. I finally looked at my friend's wife, almost daring her to say it again. And she did. But for some strange reason she wasn't looking at me. She was looking at my wife. My friend grabbed his wife's arm, but she pulled away from him and stood up. And then it all came out...Three weeks later my friend and my wife moved in together. I was looking for something that had been missing. I just didn't realize how long it'd been gone.

Notes:

Let me remind you that you are retelling this event. That means you've already experienced these emotions. They are not the same as reliving the event, though that could be a take on it.

It is very important for you to choose the unseen character and their vested interest in hearing this story. Is there any interest? Are you telling this to a stranger, a friend a new girlfriend, a colleague? Are you explaining this, years later to a son or daughter? You may think, I would never do that, but this isn't you, it's the character. What would the character do? What situation might bring that to the forefront?

The more difficult the story is, the more compelling the experience. And given any of those titles, what's the real relationship? If it's a girlfriend, is this the first date? Is this just before you plan to remarry? How long ago did the event occur? As my good friend John

Strawbridge suggests (*The Audition Book*), "Who is the last person you would tell the story to? Tell it to that person."

It's here that I must warn you about psychiatrists being the unseen character. Though psychiatrists perform a great service, they are being paid to listen. I'm not sure that anyone being paid to listen offers a very compelling story. Just after we introduced this notion in our Working Actor class, one of the cable channels began a dramatic series set in a psychiatric office. I watched a couple of the episodes. I repeat; avoid using a psychiatrist as the unseen character.

You'll notice also that the word choice and arrangement in this piece is somewhat clinical. Generally that suggests some time has passed to allow that structure to shape in memory. Perhaps that's also a somewhat of a defensive form. Your challenge is to turn something that reads more like a column into something at least somewhat conversational given the script choices you have made to define the current telling of the story.

This will be the same challenge you have as an actor when performing a corporate video script. Dialogue is somewhat more driven by the informational requirements than the conversational attributes. It will be your task to bridge the two. At least it should be.

1. To whom are you speaking?
2. Are they vested listeners?
3. Where does this conversation take place? If you are in an isolated location (two people in an apartment) you can speak at a chosen volume more freely. If you are in a public place, your volume will be dictated by what the environs necessitate and by your proximity to other people. Be specific and choose how to suggest the appropriate difference.
4. What precipitated the conversation?

5. What do you expect will follow the conversation?

One trap about retelling an incident is that it tends to take the form of a list. I did this and then this and then this and then this. It becomes tedious in form. Use your vocal vocabulary to keep the monologue alive and more rhythmic than simply reciting a list or simple time line of events.

Would You Like to Dance

Uhh…excuse me…would you like to dance? I, uhh…I can't promise you that I won't step on your feet, but it might be worth a couple spins on the floor. I'm assuming of course, you dance. But then why else would you be here. And you look like you have a dancer's legs…Oh; I hope you don't mind me noticing. Well of course, men are going to notice…I guess, I mean I hope you don't mind me saying I noticed…You're embarrassed. I'm sorry. You know what, don't say anything. Let me start this over on a better foot, so to speak. My name is Jim. My friend over there, said honesty is the best introduction. So I was honest about possibly stepping on your feet and probably too honest about your legs. But honestly, if I could have even one dance with you tonight, I think it would change my life…Oh and don't worry about the limp. I used to be a real good dancer…that was before … well anyway, this new leg is a little stiff, heh…but the rest of me is still pretty limber. So, will you…

dance with me? Uhh...Did I say my name was Jim?

Notes:

In this monologue, you'll need to decide if the character is fighting nerves or is otherwise affected in some way that impedes his emotional progress. In a college class on communication, I learned about micromomentaries. These are very fast physical behaviors that allow us to make judgments about people. Sizing people up in a blink, we (right or wrong) make these judgments every day and decide whether or not we want to engage or avoid.

This piece will depend heavily on what physical choices you make to augment the dialogue. Our understanding will come more from those choices than any decision you make about the vocal delivery.

It will thus be very important that you establish the "world" prior to uttering that first "Uhh." What choices will you make to establish the character during what is essentially the approach?

Another choice you'll need to make involves the limp. At what point should you reveal it to the audience? If you reveal it at the beginning, you'll place the audience in the same condition as the unseen character. You'll be speaking and they'll be thinking; how can you dance? If you reveal it just before the reveal in the monologue, the audience will find themselves suddenly on a different path than the one they thought they were taking. That's sometimes a very good place for them to be.

You'll also need to decide how much of a limp to effect. Should the limp suggest that the dancing will be mildly problematic or extremely difficult?

What will we learn about the unseen character? In some of these monologues, the unseen character is very real as suggested by the unheard dialogue. In this case, your character seems to be pressing on without allowing any verbal response, so we can only gain glimpses of the other character as you allow those non-verbal responses to appear during your dialogue. What will those responses be and how will they appear?

For the writer, there's much weight to be given to the chosen words and even the words that are omitted. For the actor, there's much weight to be given to the behavior and what lies at the heart of the words. You certainly have to decide how to speak the dialogue, but learn to look beyond the words and make the physical choices that communicate with their own powerful language.

AFTERWARD

How to Write Your Own Monologues

I have to mention that the title of this list has just sent chills down the spine of every auditor and casting director in America. Many actors have already attempted this with miserable results. Much like the rejected on a reality talent show, you sit and wonder, what were they thinking? Hopefully these guidelines will minimize the rejection and the poor first (and sometimes last) impressions.

1. Writing prose and dialogue are two different skills. You might try speaking your dialogue into a recorder and then transcribing. You'll be closer to a natural spoken form.
2. Don't fall in love with your work. You need to be detached enough to edit the things that may be wonderful in and of themselves, but don't work

within the context of the whole. And in case you are second guessing yourself, no; they don't work.
3. Don't ramble. Know where you're starting and where you need to end. Make sure there's a story. All compelling stories have conflict.
4. The monologue needs to be about *your* character! Why is your character telling this story?
5. Test your monologue with a coach or other actors (not necessarily a friend or someone in your type and age range). I'm sorry, it's a competitive business and you need someone to be brutally honest. Liking or disliking it is not an answer. Get specifics.
6. It's much easier to edit than to write, so don't wait. Get a sense of your story and just start. Don't wait for inspiration. Don't wait for someone to whisper in your ear. Don't wait. Write!
7. Listen to people talk. Don't follow scripted material, even material that makes it to screen is sometimes skewed. Listen to real people. Actors evidently aren't, since they're playing someone

else. At least that's what some ad agencies believe. Well, there goes that work.

8. Don't task your audience. Don't get overly emotional in 90 seconds; we won't believe it, not even when *you* do it.
9. Don't bore us. Get our attention immediately. Sometimes the evaluation is made in the first 15 seconds; certainly an opinion is formed in the first 30 seconds.
10. Know your time limit (usually 90-120 seconds) and leave us wanting more. That doesn't mean not finishing, though that's not the major crime some might suspect, but at least foster in us the desire to see more of you and perhaps wonder what happens next for your character.

Consider the idea source notes in the Introduction. Stories are everywhere. If you really enjoy writing and want to learn more, consider taking a creative writing course at your local university or community college.

Review Notes

1. Don't select a monologue that is identified with a well-known actor.
2. Is the monologue believably suitable for you (age and physical appropriateness)? It doesn't have to be realistic; it just has to be believable.
3. What does the monologue reveal about you? This is not about mimicking another actor's portrayal but exposing yourself. Some people put a character on—others open themselves up by employing past experiences, observations and depth of feeling. Will it allow you to demonstrate yourself?
4. Can the audience reasonably suspend disbelief within the time limit?
5. Why is your character telling this story?
6. Is this stream of consciousness or a retelling of an event? Is there discovery along the way or do you already know the ending?
7. Who are you talking to?

8. What is the reaction of the unseen person(s)?
9. Are you responding to that reaction? Where are the beats?
10. What came before? We need to have a sense of that before you speak a word.

What is the purpose of a monologue audition?

1. To see your physicality (height, body type, hair color, age range, etc.)
2. To hear your voice
    a. quality
    b. projection
    c. dynamics (modulation, inflection)
3. To observe stage presence (energy, engagement)
4. To see movement (including entry and exit)
5. To watch you think and listen (this isn't a recitation)
6. To see you act (consider the subtleties)

Do not confuse a monologue audition with a staged

reading for the author. Remember, this performance is not a demonstration of the monologue; it's a demonstration of you.

Merriam-Webster defines monologue as
   a. A dramatic sketch performed by one actor
   b. A long speech monopolizing conversation

1. Who are you talking to? Be specific and be able to describe this person.
2. Where are you having this monologue? Are other people there? Do they hear you?
3. Why are you telling this story?
4. What has happened or been said prior to the beginning of the monologue? Even though the monologue has a beginning, something has to precede it.
5. How does the other person react to this monologue? This may be different at different places in the piece.
6. How do you respond to the other person's reactions?

7. Have you and/or the other person changed by the end of the piece?
8. What happens after the end of the monologue?

Final approbation: Everyone has an opinion. You will need to follow the guidelines of the auditioning site and/or casting director.

But to be most effective, you will need to create a scene because:

There are no monologues; there are only dialogues for one.

ABOUT THE AUTHOR

Gary Wheeler holds an A.A. from Anne Arundel Community College, a B.A. from University of Maryland Baltimore County [where he graduated Magna Cum Laude (Phi Kappa Phi Honor Society)] and an M.A. from Towson University.

As an Adjunct Associate Professor, he's taught the following courses at institutions such as UMUC, Towson University and Anne Arundel Community College:

    Introduction to Oral Communication
    Photojournalism in a Digital Age
    Photography I
    Understanding Movies
    Film and American Culture
    TV Studio Production
    Electronic Field Production
    Introduction to Mass Communications
    Communication Theory

Mass Communication & Media Studies
Producing for Television
Lighting for the Camera
Introduction to Electronic Media

As a member of SGA-AFTRA for close to 30 years, Gary has appeared in theatrical films, network television, national commercials and corporate video.

He is one of three founding members (with John Strawbridge & Wayne Shipley) of the Actors Company Theatre, where he has directed, written and starred in several productions.

In addition to his private acting classes and coaching, he also has a full resume working as a freelance photographer, videographer and writer.

Gary was also a Toastmasters International World Championship of Public Speaking finalist and is available for speaking engagements and readings.

gary@actorsco.com

The Monologue Book

www.ingramcontent.com/pod-product-compliance
Lightning Source LLC
Chambersburg PA
CBHW071714090426
42738CB00009B/1770